A LIVING HERITAGE

RSPB Nature Reserves

Published by The Royal Society for the Protection of Birds,
The Lodge, Sandy, Bedfordshire SG19 2DL.
ISBN 0-903138-12-3
RSPB reference 42-974-00-01

Front cover: view over Irish Marshes Nature Reserve by W S Paton

Illustrations by J Busby, R Hume and D Powell

Contents

Introduction

The very idea of buying land to conserve wildlife is remarkable: firstly, that we have to do it, secondly, that we have been able to do so, with such success, since the 1930s. As support for the RSPB through its membership has steadily increased, so has its nature reserves. We now have almost 150 nature reserves, owned, leased or managed by agreement, covering over 100,000 hectares (250,000 acres).

This is impressive: but commitment is required simply to keep them going. The habitats must be managed to maintain their suitability for wildlife, and sometimes extensive restoration work is needed. The RSPB also creates new areas of specialised habitats, such as whole new reedbeds and wetlands. We have been doing this for many years, pioneering such techniques with the creation of the famous Scrape at Minsmere.

Habitat management is expensive. So are facilities for people who, having given money towards the purchase of a nature reserve, naturally wish to come and see it, to enjoy its wildness and to see the birds that benefit from its existence. Nature reserves also need staff. Much work is done by volunteers, but they cannot do all the research, surveying and work necessary to make a nature reserve run effectively. Buying the nature reserve is an important first step, but it is simply that – the bottom rung on the ladder to successful habitat management and visitor management. And all of that costs money.

Over the years, RSPB members have been magnificent in helping us to acquire and manage nature reserves, especially those who gave legacies, no matter how big or small.

Of course, nature reserves are not and never can be the complete answer to any country's conservation needs. Yet RSPB nature reserves do have a crucial role in wild bird conservation, for many species really do benefit from small areas of particular habitats being secured and managed sympathetically. And nature reserves have a special role, too, in allowing researchers to study the requirements of birds and other wildlife. Here we can find out how to restore a habitat, then use the techniques learned on other nature reserves, or on land owned by other people. Or we can simply pass on our knowledge to others who can put it to good use elsewhere.

Nature reserves have a huge role in education. Unless we educate our children to be environmentally aware, the future will be bleak. We can introduce thousands of people each year to the RSPB and its work, recruiting many more members to help us in our goals. 'Honeypot' nature reserves help people see more birds and understand more about them; while other nature reserves are maintained as quiet, undisturbed places. It would be wrong to buy land that is justifiably famous for its wild, unspoilt qualities and turn it into a busy tourist attraction; yet many places are capable of accepting visitors, often to the benefit of local communities.

As well as being vital for birds, many of our nature reserves are wonderful and valuable places for rare butterflies, dragonflies, moths, snakes and lizards or wild flowers. Many are genuine centres for biodiversity conservation – priceless gems of our wildlife heritage. This book is a celebration of their beauty and diversity. I hope you enjoy reading it.

Graham Wynne

The story so far

In days gone by, the local castle on the hill provided safety and security for the nearby population. Whenever life was threatened by attacking enemies, disease or famine, the population would pour through the castle gates, seeking sanctuary in the well-defended fortress. As soon as it was safe to do so, the people would return to the surrounding countryside. Conditions here would once more provide the habitat and environment needed for the expanding population.

Nature reserves have pretty much the same function. They provide security for species threatened in the wider countryside. When conditions again become suitable, and the environment more capable of supporting them, the species can spread from the reserve to repopulate the surrounding countryside. There are numerous examples within the RSPB's nature reserves. The marsh harrier declined to only a single breeding pair at the Minsmere Nature Reserve in Suffolk and now has a UK population exceeding 100 nests per year from Scotland to the south coast. The avocet, which first recolonised the East Anglian coast on Havergate Island, has now spread from Humberside to Dorset and numbers over 400 pairs. The corncrake, once widespread throughout the UK, has retreated to the Western Isles and is now showing signs of recovery as the result of significant land management on RSPB nature reserves and elsewhere. In all cases, the species concerned have recovered only as a result of the wider countryside becoming suitable as a habitat.

Nature reserves did not feature in the RSPB's conservation armoury until the Society had been in operation for some 40 years. Even then, with limited resources, the acquisition of reserves was of low priority and the estate small. It sprang from a system of 'watchers' employed around the country to safeguard rare breeding species or colonies. Many watchers worked part-time, being paid a retainer by the RSPB while continuing with their own profession. They included farmers, fishermen and sometimes gamekeepers. The first was at Loch Leven, Kinross, protecting the nesting pintails in the early 1900s – now the site of the RSPB's Vane Farm Nature Reserve. Others were employed in Shetland and Orkney and at Dungeness, Kent, where the nesting seabird colonies and Kentish plovers were under threat from disturbance. The latter site is the longest established RSPB nature reserve, which we acquired in 1932.

Some of the earliest nature reserves resulted from gifts which proved to be unsuitable. A small site at Cheyne Court on Romney Marsh, Kent, was so narrow and so disturbed by surrounding activities that the Society eventually abandoned it. This has changed with the passage of time and

Authors

Bob Scott *commenced his career with the RSPB in 1960, as warden of the Dungeness Nature Reserve , where he managed the major wetland creation that resulted in the successful establishment of tern colonies. After a few years as warden at Northward Hill, Bob transferred to The Lodge where he was Head of Reserves Management. Bob retired from the RSPB in April 1997.*

Gareth Thomas *has worked for the RSPB since 1967, when he first joined the Research Department. Since 1986, he has been involved with reserves and advisory work. He is now responsible for the Land Agency, Reserves Ecology and Conservation Management Advice Departments.*

C H Gomersall (RSPB Images)

Abernethy Forest – one of the RSPB's finest and most beautiful nature reserves

5

it is now part of a successful, much larger reserve operated by another conservation organisation.

C H Gomersall (RSPB Images)

Some reserves are bought specifically to protect extremely rare birds like the roseate tern

From the first acquisition in 1932, through to the end of the 1950s, nature reserves were few and the Society had no policy for building up its portfolio. Nonetheless, the 10 reserves acquired by 1960 included such important and well-known sites as Minsmere; Havergate Island; Grassholm, Pembrokeshire, with its massive gannet colony; and Northward Hill, Kent, with its colony of grey herons. During this period, there was no proven background of site protection within the UK. Legislation providing for National Nature Reserves and Sites of Special Scientific Interest was in its infancy.

The 1960s saw the first real growth in the RSPB acquiring reserves where species were under immediate threat. These included sites such as Inchmickery in the Firth of Forth for the nesting roseate terns; Leighton Moss, Lancashire, for the breeding bitterns; Fetlar, Shetland, for the red-necked phalaropes and snowy owls that had started nesting; the Ouse Washes in Cambridgeshire for the recolonising black-tailed godwits; Arne, Dorset, for the Dartford warblers; and Loch Garten (now Abernethy), Highlands, for the recolonising ospreys. By 1970, the RSPB owned or held by lease or agreement 31 nature reserves.

The 1970s and 1980s saw some dramatic changes both within and outside the RSPB. Massive changes were taking place in land

management and agriculture throughout the UK. Conservation and environmental organisations recorded exceptional increases in their membership and a range of organisations became involved in reserve acquisition and management. The concept of managing land for wildlife as opposed to simply protecting it for wildlife had slowly developed during the 1960s.

As part of these changes, the RSPB saw its membership rise from 10,000 in 1960 to over 100,000 by the early 1970s. The increased resources and support led to yet further reserve acquisition. Forty-four new nature reserves were acquired in the 1970s, including Titchwell Marsh, Norfolk; Elmley Marshes, Kent; Rathlin Island Cliffs, Co Antrim; Insh Marshes, Highland; and West Sedgemoor, Somerset. In addition, with members' support and successful appeals for money, it proved possible to buy Minsmere and Loch Garten, which until then were only managed by agreement with their owners. At times, the reserves mechanism was called upon to act in emergency circumstances. Wolves Wood in Suffolk was purchased from under the blades of bulldozers that were starting to clear the site.

The growth continued in the 1980s and 1990s, but by this time the Society was becoming more focused as to priorities for species and habitats. Considerations included the degree of threat to important or priority habitats; which were the most important species or collection of species needing reserve protection; and where could the still precious financial resources be best directed. Buying nature reserves is expensive. Land that once cost £15–20 per acre now commands over £2,000 per acre. Managing a site to maintain its conservation potential can cost tens of thousands of pounds per annum. Nature reserves have become larger and more sophisticated as the RSPB has concentrated on national and international priorities.

Acquisitions included Loch Gruinart, Islay (over 1,600 ha) for its wintering geese and more recently, corncrakes; Abernethy Forest, Highlands (over 12,700 ha) for Caledonian pinewoods and the capercaillie; and Forsinard in the Flow Country of the Highlands (over 7,100 ha) for the unique peatlands and nesting northern waders.

By 1997, the RSPB was managing almost 150 sites throughout the UK, covering 100,000 ha (250,000 acres). These range from the most northerly, Fetlar in the Shetland Islands, to the most southerly, Marazion Marsh, Cornwall; from the most westerly, Lower Lough Erne Islands, Co Fermanagh, to the most easterly, Berney Marshes and Breydon Water, Norfolk. Although the average size of an RSPB reserve is about 700 ha, they range from a tiny, half-hectare (one acre) tern island to the large native Caledonian pinewood estate at Abernethy Forest, which covers almost 13,000 ha (32,045 acres).

RSPB nature reserves cover several habitats which amount to a significant proportion of the UK total. The 1,950 ha (4,800 acres) of reedswamps and fen on RSPB reserves represents 24% of the UK resource of this habitat and provides breeding sites for 10 pairs of bitterns (50% of the UK population).

The 4,850 ha (11,955 acres) of lowland wet grassland on 21 nature reserves, now represents 24% of this habitat in the UK that is still flooded regularly. These nature reserves provide nesting sites for up to 26 pairs of black-tailed godwits (up to 91% of the UK population) and wintering grounds for over 83,000 wigeons (50% of the UK population) and up to 450 bean geese (up to 80% of the UK population).

The nature reserve at Abernethy Forest holds almost 2,000 ha (4,930 acres) of native Caledonian pine, which is almost 15% of the remaining area of this very scarce habitat. A major programme of deer management,

which is reducing grazing pressure, is allowing new areas of pinewood to regenerate. This habitat is an important last refuge for many species of conservation concern, including the capercaillie, crested tit and Scottish crossbill. We hope these species will colonise other areas of native Scots pine which we hope will be further encouraged in the surrounding countryside.

R Wilmshurst (FLPA)

The bearded tit is an attractive bird of reedbeds. Its presence is often revealed by its unusual 'pinging' call

RSPB members have always helped us to acquire new nature reserves, whether by leaving a legacy to the RSPB, such as that for Pulborough, or by responding to our appeals – we couldn't do it without them. The RSPB's most ambitious and most successful appeal was in 1988 to acquire the Highland estate at Abernethy Forest. This has since become a flagship reserve in the battle to create more native Caledonian pinewood in Scotland. Our appeals have also been supported with successful grant applications to the Heritage Lottery Fund, English Nature, Countryside Council for Wales, Scottish Natural Heritage, Department of the Environment (Northern Ireland), and the Countryside Commission, together with a number of private charitable trusts.

Sand lizard

Through the 1990s, the RSPB has continued to buy new land costing some £2 million each year. The annual management costs for maintaining the correct habitats on the RSPB's 140 nature reserves now amount to some £6 million each year. This sum includes providing facilities for RSPB members and other visitors to come and see the birds and glimpse the management regimes needed to support them.

Heathlands are vital to the future of the sand lizard, one of our rarest reptiles

Opposite page: barn owl over Titchwell Marsh

C H Gomersall (RSPB Images)

RSPB nature reserves contribute to conserving the whole range of wildlife. Their management is designed to safeguard those species that are considered 'red data' or threatened in the UK. The Scottish primrose is found nowhere else in the world but the north of Scotland. It grows at the Forsinard Nature Reserve. The world population of the endemic spathulate fleawort is confined to South Stack, Anglesey – an RSPB nature reserve. The high brown fritillary is a butterfly that has declined in distribution by about 94% over the last 40 years. There is a stronghold at Leighton Moss, Lancashire. Marsh fritillaries are declining rapidly in north-west Europe and the RSPB has a stronghold at Loch Gruinart, Islay. The RSPB Strumpshaw Fen Nature Reserve in Norfolk is host to the swallowtail butterfly whose caterpillars feed on milk parsley, itself a scarce plant.

Sand lizards, one of the UK's rarest reptiles, depend on the management of

Corncrake

heaths in southern England. They breed in sandy areas, often alongside visitor paths, on the RSPB's heathland reserve of Arne, Dorset. The shingle at Dungeness has some 37 species of moths and 35 species of beetle that are of national importance. This nature reserve has also recorded 12 species of bumble bee (long since gone from the surrounding land) and is the only known site in the world for a species of leaf hopper. Also, in some of the water areas on Dungeness, it is possible to find large populations of the rare medicinal leech.

Management programmes for many threatened birds have been devised after extensive research projects at RSPB nature reserves. Over the years, management techniques for conserving such species as Dartford warblers, bitterns, corncrakes, terns, waders and wintering wildfowl have been tested on the RSPB's reserves. Subsequently, many of these techniques have been adopted elsewhere and often help form the basis for government environmental subsidy schemes such as Environmentally Sensitive Areas (ESAs). The range of management carried out on RSPB nature reserves means that they are ideal for demonstrating techniques to land-use advisers both here and abroad. Over a two year period, the RSPB has held over 40 training sessions on its nature reserves, involving people from as far afield as the USA, Sierra Leone and Tanzania. RSPB reserve staff, especially wardens and ecologists, are also in demand to advise on practical conservation overseas. They have helped draw up management plans for important bird areas in many countries.

What of the future? Conditions in the wider countryside are not getting any better. Wetlands continue to be drained, uplands continue to be overgrazed, land claims continue to threaten prime areas of estuaries and lowland heath. Rising sea levels threaten areas of intertidal mud and saltmarsh which are refuges for

internationally important numbers of wintering waterfowl. The RSPB is committed to build upon the flagship nature reserves that have been established on estuaries and wetlands, particularly in England; to acquire some of the best areas of the Flow Country, Sutherland; and to manage a chain of sites for the recovery of the corncrake. Much still remains to be done to save and create wet lowland grassland in Northern Ireland and other parts of lowland Britain. More reedbeds need to be created in England and Wales for breeding bitterns.

Other species in need of help include the stone-curlew, whose numbers are balanced precariously at 150 pairs. With the apparent continuation of the decline in 'common' farmland birds, what other species will next need the help of RSPB nature reserves? It seems incredible that we would ever need reserves for such widespread species as skylarks or linnets, but the time may not be far off. Already special areas have had to be provided to help once widespread species such as the cirl bunting and corncrake. In the next millennium, the RSPB may need some nature reserves on farmland and in the uplands to help develop better management techniques. Together with other landowning bodies, there may yet be another series of castles to build to help shelter the more beleaguered species. Not all will be successful, but for many species and certain habitats, it will be one of the few chances they have of maintaining themselves in an ever-developing UK.

Gareth Thomas.

L Campbell (NHPA)

Sunset over Loch Gruinart

Opposite page: ospreys – the pride of Loch Garten

Managing reserves the RSPB way

Many habitats deteriorate without appropriate management and so most nature reserves need some degree of physical management to maintain their conservation interest. Put another way, there is more to conservation management than putting a fence around an area and calling it a nature reserve.

Many of the birds which we regard as special, such as bitterns, avocets and Dartford warblers, depend on habitats which are at an early successional stage. Without intervention by the reserve manager, the original habitats would change progressively into others which would be unsuitable for the birds which we are trying to conserve. For example, without appropriate management, avocet lagoons would become overgrown with reeds and other rank vegetation which would in turn become alder or willow carr and eventually mature woodland. For this reason, RSPB wardens and volunteers spend countless hours trying to suspend or halt the succession by, for example, removing invading birch and pine from lowland heathland or invading willow from reedbeds.

The more mature a habitat is, the less intense the management needs to be. Thus, newly-formed islands of mud or shingle need regular weeding to maintain their attractiveness to nesting avocets. Conversely, high forest with abundant dead wood needs no particular physical management, least of all the removal of mature or dying trees which provide food and nest sites for woodpeckers.

Management can be very time-consuming and expensive, but for some habitats the warden is able to delegate the task to willing volunteers – otherwise known as domestic stock, such as cattle or sheep. The acquisition and management of nature reserves is a long-term commitment not to be undertaken lightly. To justify the great expense of reserves management (currently running at over £6 million per annum), sites must be managed effectively with tangible benefits.

Each RSPB nature reserve has a management plan which is the framework within which all future work of the site is planned and carried out. It describes and evaluates the importance of the site, identifies the aims and objectives of management, the work needed to achieve these objectives and the monitoring required to assess the success of management and how it could be improved.

C H Gomersall (RSPB Images)

Authors

Graham Hirons *joined the RSPB as a reserves ecologist in 1989. Since 1993, he has been Head of Reserves Ecology in the RSPB's Conservation Management Department. He is responsible for overseeing the preparation of management plans for reserves, the provision of ecological advice to managers and wardens, biological recording on reserves, and monitoring results of management.*

Geoffrey Osborn *is Head of Land Agency at The Lodge, the department responsible for all reserve acquisitions, for all building projects on reserves and for advising on management, especially farming, forestry and other such activities. He is a chartered surveyor and has worked for the RSPB for seven years, prior to which he gained experience in management of agricultural estates in the West Country and the Midlands.*

Most nature reserves need some degree of physical management

Opposite page: Bempton Cliffs

The management plan enables anyone to understand how and why decisions are taken by stating what, when, where, why and how management is to be carried out. This can be especially useful when explaining our management to visitors or the local community. The plan also ensures a measure of continuity in the event of the warden being run over by the proverbial bus!

The avocet, symbol of the RSPB

C H Gomersall (RSPB Images)

Nature reserve management is still regarded by many, with some justification, as an art not a science. This is because the nesting and feeding requirements of many birds and the interactions between different plant and animal species and communities are very complex, and not well understood. RSPB staff and volunteers spend much time surveying and monitoring the habitat and species management to ensure that the conservation value of reserves is being maintained or enhanced as planned. Monitoring is important for all species

and habitats but especially for rare and endangered species. It is also important for fast-growing or aggressive plant or animal species such as bracken on moorland or gull colonies on tern islands. It's not only important to look at the effectiveness of different types of management, but also to research the food and habitat requirements of birds in order that management can be improved.

Although the RSPB acquires and manages land primarily to help further its bird conservation aims, its reserves are not called 'nature reserves' without good reason. Because they are spread throughout the UK and contain a wide range of semi-natural habitats, including many of the scarcer ones like heathland and native pine forest, the reserves support a rich variety of plants and animals in addition to birds. Indeed, a quarter of RSPB nature reserves qualify as Sites of Special Scientific Interest (SSSIs) on botanical grounds alone. For this reason, all RSPB reserves are managed for their intrinsic nature conservation value, where management for birds is integrated with other important nature conservation goals. Whenever appropriate, advice on management for groups other than birds is sought from experts and specialists such as Butterfly Conservation and the British Dragonfly Society.

The expansion of intensive farming, urban areas and industrial development, particularly in lowland Britain, has meant that there are relatively few unprotected areas of outstanding wildlife interest left to conserve and we are beginning to run out of prime wildlife habitat to acquire as nature reserves. For this reason, the RSPB is looking increasingly towards re-creating lost habitats or restoring the wildlife value of damaged or degraded sites. The RSPB is undertaking exciting new projects to create significant areas of new reedbed for breeding bitterns in East Anglia, south-west England and Wales, heathland for stone-curlews and woodlarks in East Anglia, coastal pools for avocets in south-east England and restoring wet grasslands throughout the UK to benefit breeding lapwings and snipe and wintering geese and ducks.

Over the years, the RSPB has had many management successes where our input has seen visible improvements in the number of species in a particular area. Probably one of the most impressive has been at Pulborough Brooks. Raising water levels, controlled flooding and summer cattle grazing has resulted in the number of wintering waterfowl going up from a few hundred when we first bought the reserve in 1989 to over 15,000 in 1996.

We have also been working hard to save some of the last remaining areas of Caledonian pine forests. At Abernethy, deer have been controlled to allow new trees to establish which has had a startling effect at the forest edge – the forest is expanding, perhaps for the first time in centuries. Black grouse have also begun to benefit and capercaillies displaying at their traditional lek sites have doubled.

Managing and restoring heathland on some of our nature reserves has also seen tremendous benefits, not only to birds but to endangered species such as sand lizards and smooth snakes. And heathland ponds, dug out to provide habitat for rare dragonflies, also provide a water supply for fighting heathland fires. At Minsmere, 158 ha (380 acres) of arable land is being restored to heathland and acid grassland for the benefit of stone-curlews and woodlarks.

Because most mammals are active only at night, visitors might be surprised to learn that 54 species of mammal (plus 10 species of whale and dolphin offshore) have been recorded on RSPB nature reserves, including 41 of the 44 species native to

C Carver (RSPB Images)

Smooth snakes are found on three RSPB heathland reserves

Britain. Otters have been recorded on no less than 57 nature reserves and breed on 17, but they are probably most easily seen by visitors at Leighton Moss. Among the rarer species, red squirrels occur at 13 nature reserves, dormice at 11, pine martens at six and polecats at five.

All six amphibian and six reptile species that are native to the UK occur on RSPB nature reserves, including the four threatened species, the smooth snake and sand lizard (both found on three reserves), the natterjack toad (one reserve and successfully introduced to two others) and the great crested newt (nine reserves).

Forty-six of the 55 species of British butterflies are found on RSPB nature reserves. This list includes three vulnerable red data species, the swallowtail (Mid Yare), high brown fritillary (Leighton Moss) and heath fritillary (Blean Woods), and nine nationally notable species. Maintaining woodland rides and glades and the traditional coppicing that is carried out on many nature reserves have improved conditions for woodland butterflies. Butterflies on reserves have also benefited from the removal of scrub from dry grassland, fen and heathland habitats. A standardised national scheme for monitoring butterfly numbers is organised by the Institute of Terrestrial Ecology and operates on 36 nature reserves.

Green woodpecker

Eighty-nine per cent of the 726 species of British macro-moths are found on RSPB nature reserves including 183 (71%) of the red data and nationally notable species. No less than 35 of the 38 species of dragonflies native to Britain and Ireland breed on RSPB nature reserves. They include all six threatened species listed in the red data book for British insects. The improvement of water quality that occurs with reserve management, together with wetland creation and restoration has resulted in many reserves now holding nationally important dragonfly populations. Arne in Dorset has recorded the largest number of species (29).

Over half of the RSPB's nature reserves have at least one nationally rare or scarce plant species. Twenty-nine (9%) of Britain's red data species and 46% of nationally scarce species occur on RSPB nature reserves. These include endemic species (ie unique to Britain), such as the nationally scarce Scottish primrose which thrives at North Hill, Papa Westray in Orkney;

endemic subspecies such as the spathulate fleawort, a distinct form of field fleawort with fleshy leaves unique to the maritime cliffs around the RSPB's South Stack Nature Reserve; and plants at the limit of their botanical range in Europe like the pale forget-me-not found in Britain only on the Cumbrian nature reserves of Geltsdale and Haweswater. The most important reserve for plants is Abernethy with no less than seven red data and 41 nationally scarce species including many arctic alpines.

Clearly, careful management of nature reserves brings about success for breeding birds and other wildlife. It's an expensive business, but one we feel really is at the heart of conservation.

Geoffrey Osborn

Graham Hirons

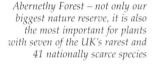

Abernethy Forest – not only our biggest nature reserve, it is also the most important for plants with seven of the UK's rarest and 41 nationally scarce species

D Tomlinson (RSPB Images)

Exploring the mouth of the river

There can be few places left outside the Scottish glens and flows or a piece of ancient forest that can give as great a sense of sheer 'nature' as the wide open space of an estuary.

They are magical places, touching all of the senses: that distinctive smell of damp mud or seaweed; the feel of wind on your face; the sight of the clouds and the sunset, or of rain sweeping across the skyline; the taste of the wind-borne salt from the sea; and of course the sound of the birds – feeding, roosting, flying or just chatting – sometimes mixed with the distant chugging of a boat.

Estuaries need us as much as we need them. They need our constraint, our protection and our tolerance. We need them for their solitude, their peace and for thousands of birds to feed and roost in safety.

And these magical places can be found all around the country – in fact all around the world!

History

Estuaries form in two ways. Firstly, rivers like the Severn, the Humber, the Exe and the Dee slow down in their last stages, depositing their mud and mixing their freshwater with the seawater, before meeting the sea. A second type, like the Stour, Orwell and Blackwater in East Anglia, was formed after the last ice age. During this period, the freshwater had been locked up in the ice sheets that covered most of the northern hemisphere. When these melted, the land sank and sea levels rose by tens of metres, drowning out the low-lying valleys.

This ancient landscape was very different from today. Most eastern rivers were

D Woodfall (Woodfall Wild Images)

Flat, but not featureless, estuaries like the Dee are teeming with wading birds and wildfowl in winter

tributaries of the Thames which itself was a tributary of the Rhine. With the massive rise in sea level after successive ice ages, the forests that joined us to Holland were drowned out. An enormous waterfall is believed to have broken the land tie in the Dover area, making us an island. This stopped terrestrial animals moving and colonising the new landscape, but of course it didn't stop the birds.

The erosion of the new landscape in the east and the old landscape of the west formed millions of tons of silts and muds. The rivers brought these down to the sea and deposited them, creating mudflats and eventually saltmarsh.

Tides

The estuary mudflats are covered by a regular cycle of two high tides a day – usually 12 hours apart and an hour later each day. The moon affects the height of the tides, which vary during the lunar month.

Author

Richard Powell *joined the RSPB in 1988 as Reserves Manager, East Anglia. He was promoted to Regional Manager for East Anglia in 1994. Before joining the RSPB, Richard worked for MAFF before taking a degree in geology.*

A major influence on the UK's seas is the Gulf Stream, that sweeps warm water in from the Atlantic. As it moves up the west coast, the water is still relatively warm. But as it sweeps across the north of Scotland and mixes with the Arctic Ocean current, it chills so that the water moving down the east coast to the English Channel is much colder. A human falling off an oil rig or ship off the north-east coast can survive as little as two minutes in winter and only about 10 minutes later in the year!

Common terns fly 6,000 miles from Africa to spend the summer here. Many feed on estuaries such as the Dee

G Smith (RSPB Images)

The Gulf Stream also sweeps past Cornwall and up the English Channel. When it converges on Avonmouth in the Bristol Channel, it produces the second highest tidal range in the world – over 12 metres.

Food
It has been estimated that, on an average estuary, each square metre of mud produces the equivalent food value of 15 Mars Bars per year. Our biggest estuary, the Wash, covers 600,000,000 square metres – or nine billion Mars Bars!

These rich feeding grounds attract millions of birds. Because the UK's estuaries do not usually freeze, they are open for feeding all year. This makes them vital resting and feeding places for birds migrating north and south.

Estuaries are ideal for fish to spawn and as nurseries for young fish. These are food for cormorants and saw-billed ducks such as mergansers and goosanders. The water and mud are rich in invertebrates and the twice daily exposure and covering of the mud by the tide create excellent feeding grounds for wading birds.

Waders have various bill shapes and sizes that fit them for different ways of feeding. The long curved beak of the curlew is perfect to probe deep into the mud for the larger burrowing prey such as ragworms and lugworms. Sanderlings, on the other hand, scurry along the edge of the tide picking up pieces with their small beaks. Between these two extremes are birds such as redshanks, oystercatchers, turnstones and knots. Each species exploits the area of the estuary best suited to its needs. Their numbers and distribution help to identify the most important areas to protect for feeding birds.

Nowadays, pollution can greatly reduce the food available to birds. Episodes like the oil spills in the Mersey and off the coast of Pembrokeshire cause severe damage to the invertebrates living in the mud. Oil comes in different thicknesses. All cause damage – but heavy crude oils like those from the Gulf States, which are used in power stations or in ship engines, cause the most. They sink to the bottom, blanketing out the mud and killing the invertebrates as well as other animal and plant life. It can take at least five years for the habitat to recover from such an incident. In the meantime, the birds have to try to find somewhere else to feed.

Birds of estuaries

There are 24 estuaries in the UK that are internationally important to birds. Each of these regularly holds over 20,000 birds, and some of them many more than that number. The RSPB has always recognised the importance of estuaries and has spent a lot of time researching into estuary ecology, management, disturbance, zoning, planning and bird counts. And, of course, we buy reserves on the important ones whenever possible, to safeguard or enhance threatened areas.

Birds need large, undisturbed areas in which to feed. Constant disruption by people, dogs, boats or jet skis can be fatal, especially when the birds are facing other pressures, such as winter cold. Disturbing roosting or feeding birds has been likened to waking someone in the middle of the night and forcing them to run around the block – and then repeating this up to six or seven times a night. With such disturbance, birds are also unable to feed and quickly become very weak, so please take care next time you visit an estuary.

On a rising tide you can get spectacular views of birds close up. Some sites, such as Snettisham on the Wash in Norfolk, are particularly awe-inspiring. On spring tides, there can be over 100,000 birds pushed on to the nature reserve as the last of the mud is covered. The sight and sound of, say, 50,000 knots, 25,000 oystercatchers, 13,000 dunlins, 7,000 bar-tailed godwits and 1,000 grey plovers flying overhead is pure emotion. They collect over the estuary like plumes of smoke. As they get closer, the cloud changes from black to silver as they

wheel round and round before coming down to the pits. They rest here at high tide and then, as it falls, they move once more onto the mud to feed. Other estuaries such as Morecambe Bay can offer wader spectacles, but none can match Snettisham.

C H Gomersall (RSPB Images)

Dense flocks of knots are a familiar high tide spectacle on the Wash

Wild geese of all sorts also enjoy the open space and food offered by estuaries. They range from the rare to the common or introduced. Many come south from the Arctic and Russia, stopping on our unfrozen estuaries to winter or to stock up with food after a long flight. In Northern Ireland, you will see the light-bellied brent geese rather than the darker eastern race, along with Greenland white-fronted and barnacle geese. Along the east coast of Britain, the brent geese are the dark-bellied variety and you can also see pink-footed geese, as well as greylag and Canada geese, both of which were introduced to this country.

The birds need to find secure places to roost. If there are no convenient RSPB or other nature reserves, then they have to find alternatives. Sometimes this is on natural saltmarsh, other times on

M Lane (Woodfall Wild Images)

More than half of the UK's redshanks breed on estuaries

Brent geese

and by Sandwich terns with their distinctive crests and black bills with yellow tips. Havergate Island in the Ore Estuary in Suffolk is one of the best places to see Sandwich terns, but they are present all around our coasts. Sandwich terns are the largest terns seen regularly in the UK.

Gulls, especially black-headed, breed in large numbers on many estuaries. There may be thousands of these noisy and argumentative birds, and you will certainly hear the colony before you see it. More timid species such as terns and sometimes avocets will be mixed in with these, seeking protection among the big noisy colonies. However, the gulls may predate the nests or chicks of other species.

Saltmarshes and their birds

Estuaries also hold another threatened habitat – saltmarsh. Saltmarshes are formed over the centuries by the build up of muds. Their top surface is only covered occasionally by really high tides. These occasions can range from a few times a year to once in five, 10 or even 25 years – giving rise to different plant communities in different areas.

Saltmarshes trap sediment from the water which would otherwise fill the channels. They also put important organic matter back into the estuary, as well as flies and other insects which are food for the fish.

Saltmarshes add a magical element to estuaries. As well as bringing greenness and, in autumn, pinks, reds and purples to this wide open space, they are also important breeding grounds for birds. Although only about nine bird species breed on saltmarsh, they do so in high numbers. For example, estuaries around Britain may hold over 18,000 breeding redshanks – approximately one-fifth of Europe's breeding population and over half of all those breeding in the UK. They must be protected.

agricultural fields. Along the Thames, where there is particular pressure from building and development, the birds even roost in car parks!

Estuaries in winter tend to be cold and windy. To some people, this desolation is their attraction, but the cold can take its toll on the birds. If the top layer of mud is frozen for a period of time, the smaller beaked birds find it hard to feed and the probing birds can't probe.

As winter loosens its grip, the wintering birds move north and the birds from warmer climes like Africa come to take their place. Terns call as they fish the shallower waters for small fish and eels. Most of them come here from West Africa, 6,000 miles away.

The common tern, with its red bill, will make use of platforms where these are provided either by the RSPB or by local people – on Breydon Water on the Norfolk Broads, 75 or 80 may nest on each platform. These birds feed on the estuary and out to sea, where they are sometimes joined by little terns with their yellow bills

Redshanks, as the name suggests, are smart little birds with red legs or 'shanks' and a distinctive haunting 'TEU-hu-hu' cry. The tussocky vegetation of Britain's saltmarshes is ideal for the redshank to make its nest in a small depression. The nest and eggs are very well camouflaged and it is usually the redshank calling in anger or alarm that gives away its nest. Inevitably some nests are caught by the tide and occasionally washed away. If this happens early enough in the season, the birds will try again. Redshank eggs can be covered with seawater for an hour or so and still survive in their cup-shaped nest, but other saltmarsh birds can find their nests and eggs destroyed.

Saltmarsh vegetation is lush in summer. Grazing helps to manage it to benefit breeding birds and wintering ducks and geese. Grazing by cattle produces the uneven sward preferred by nesting redshanks as well as wintering geese. Sheep are used on Morecambe Bay and wherever less damaging feet and close grazing are needed.

D Fox (OSF)

Particular plants may attract particular birds to feed, breed or roost. Samphire (picked and eaten as a vegetable in some areas), sea aster and sea lavender provide seeds in the autumn on which wintering flocks of teals and wigeons feed avidly. These birds are fascinating to watch as they pick up seeds in their bills and then run down to the pools or creek edges to collect water to wash them down. Processions of ducks waddling back and forth at speed is an amusing sight.

Wildfowl will nest in the ditches and creeks on the higher marshes, away from the tides. Shelducks are 'not quite a duck, not quite a goose' in size. With their coloured plumage and bill, they are very visible birds on estuaries all year round. They will nest on some saltmarshes when the vegetation is dense enough, although they prefer old rabbit burrows or a space under a hide! Gulls, terns, avocets and even lapwings nest on saltmarshes and the calls of these birds are as impressive as those of the wintering flocks from October to March. But the sweetest sound of the upper saltmarsh is the song of the skylark – best heard when dozing in the long grass of the sea wall with your hat pulled down over your eyes. Geese use saltmarshes in large numbers. On the Wash, tens of thousands of pink-footed geese will be feeding or roosting by Christmas. Many of the brent geese will be on the grazing marshes behind the sea wall. Other nature reserves good for viewing dark-bellied brent geese are Holkham National Nature Reserve in North Norfolk and Langstone Harbour in Sussex.

Old Hall, an RSPB nature reserve on the Blackwater Estuary in Essex, has grazing marshes that are managed especially for geese: 5,000–7,000 birds feed here instead of on the farmers' winter cereals. To the geese, winter cereals are a nutritious meal, much like the eel grass they used to eat. This grass has been lost from many estuaries through pollution and saltmarsh erosion.

Sea aster flowers on saltmarshes. In winter, its seeds are food for wigeons and teals

Another frequent winter visitor to saltmarshes, especially on the east coast, is the twite. Known as the mountain linnet, this small bird breeds high up in the Scottish Highlands, coming to coastal sites like Frampton, Snettisham and Titchwell in winter. They tend to form flocks with skylarks and linnets to eat the saltmarsh seeds. If you are really lucky, the flock will also have shorelarks and snow buntings. Snow buntings are very 'tame' and will move just in front of you as you walk, leapfrogging over each other.

In conclusion

Despite all the pressures on estuaries and saltmarshes, they still remain magical places of solitude, nature and birds. Many people enjoy estuaries for all sorts of reasons, not least children, who can always find shells, crabs, seaweed, mermaids' purses, and a whole host of other exciting 'treasures'. Estuaries can foster a childhood interest in wildlife and nature conservation that can last a lifetime. In fact, playing as a child on Breydon Water is what sparked off my interest and led to my career in the world of conservation. My teacher at junior school told us what all the creatures were and I spent time through the summer and winter watching things come and go with the tide and the seasons.

The wide open spaces of estuaries give them a charm all of their own. Visit one near you and experience that magic – you are sure to be touched by it. Wrap up warm in winter, take some emergency chocolate and go for a long walk!

Richard Powell

Snettisham is a place of big skies and flaming sunsets

C H Gomersall (RSPB Images)

Peering through the reeds

An extensive stand of gently swaying reed is an evocative sight. To the birdwatcher, the experience is heightened by the special and elusive birds that occupy this habitat; the rare bittern with its foghorn boom, the ground-dwelling water rail shattering the silence with its explosive squeal, a group of bearded tits flitting through the reed heads, or a marsh harrier quartering the reeds. All these species are specialists, dependent on this unique habitat, which is threatened but well represented on RSPB nature reserves.

Reed is a remarkably adaptable plant. Although it is intolerant of much water movement and is principally a lowland species, most commonly associated with nutrient-rich water, it will also grow successfully in brackish water as at Blacktoft Sands Nature Reserve. It is the tallest European grass, reaching a height of up to two metres. During the main growing season of mid-April to mid-July, it grows at the rate of around two centimetres a day. This incredible growth is one of the factors that makes the habitat so interesting; a reedbed in the growing season almost literally changes in front of one's eyes. The new green growth submerges the dead brown reed of previous years, followed in quick succession by the bronzing of the whole bed as the flowers appear, then the turning of the pale fluffy heads as the seed sets.

The ability of reed to grow in water up to one metre in depth means that other plants cannot easily compete in such situations; in these wetter areas, usually only reedmace and iris occur in any quantity. In drier situations, around the edge of the reedbed, a richly varied mixed fen community develops. This varies in species from site to site. In some areas there is a marked zone dominated by sedge and rush while, in the

D Kjaer (RSPB Images)

drier sites, carr woodland, usually of willow, develops but at times alder, alder buckthorn and guelder rose may be present. All these habitats are in effect temporary or transitional. They are just one stage in the natural succession from shallow open water to oak/ash woodland which follows the carr woodland. This can happen quickly. The fast growth of the reeds quickly produces debris, where other plants can root and grow. In drier reedbeds, such as at Minsmere, the change from open water to willow woodland can take as little as 30 to 40 years, whereas in wetter reedbeds, such at Leighton Moss, it may take up to 100 years. The only way to retain the area as a suitable habitat for its rare bird inhabitants is to undertake dynamic management.

Normally hard to see, the water rail ventures into the open in winter, looking for unfrozen water

Author

John Wilson *has been warden of Leighton Moss and Morecambe Bay Nature Reserve since it started in 1964. He has written several papers on waders, reedbed birds and butterflies. For services to nature conservation he was awarded the BEM in 1991 and an honourary degree from Lancaster University in 1988.*

In total, RSPB nature reserves have almost 800 ha (2,000 acres) of reedbeds. These vary in size from a reed-filled dyke to over 120 ha (290 acres) of almost continuous reed. The largest are at Strumpshaw Fen and Surlingham Church Marsh, with Minsmere coming a close second.

One intriguing factor is that, although reed is the dominant plant, every reedbed is surprisingly different. Blacktoft Sands in Humberside is exclusively a tidal reedbed. Reed encroached on the intertidal mud after a training wall was constructed in the 1920s to contain the River Humber. There is little plant diversity within the reedbed, which is bordered by small areas of saltmarsh and couch grass. The only permanent pools or scrub areas are those formed in recent years by the RSPB's management. Despite a small range of invertebrates, fish and amphibians, the nature reserve has a thriving population of both bearded tits and marsh harriers, which colonised the site in the 1960s.

The brilliant emerald is one of the most striking dragonflies hunting over reedbeds for unsuspecting prey

of it. Reedmace, willowherb, willows, elderberry and some water weeds moved in and the range of invertebrates has increased markedly. The greater mobility of birds saw them colonise the area quickly, with both marsh harriers and bitterns nesting in the first year after the change. Bearded tits also moved to the freshwater marsh and shovelers and gadwalls took up roost.

Minsmere's reedbeds, formed when the area was flooded in 1940 as part of the coastal anti-invasion measures, are now completely fresh, protected from the sea by a ridge of sand dunes. Plant diversity is good, especially along the dry reed edge and in the smaller reedbeds close to the brackish pools. The low rainfall at Minsmere speeds up the drying out process of natural succession. Careful management has helped slow this down, resulting in an increase in the numbers of bitterns. A peak of eight marsh harrier nests in one year has also occurred, a far cry from the 1960s and early 70s when the nature reserve supported the only British breeding pair. Bearded tits and Savi's and Cetti's warblers have bred. The recently introduced otters have thrived, with two breeding pairs at present.

Although the reedbeds at Leighton Moss are freshwater, they have a much higher rainfall than those at Minsmere, slowing down the natural succession. Large beds of yellow flag and reedmace flank the reeds and summer reed cutting has improved plant variety. Bitterns, marsh harriers and bearded tits all breed, along with a population of water rails. Otters and red deer use the reedbeds regularly.

Strumpshaw and Surlingham Church Marshes are much older reedbeds. They are believed to have been formed, like the rest of the Broads, by medieval peat diggings. They have the most diverse flora of all the RSPB reedbeds, including such

Excluding tidal influences on a reedbed increases the variety of wildlife which thrives in it. Titchwell Marsh was originally all intertidal, but in 1980, a bank was built to exclude the tide from a portion

C H Gomersall (RSPB Images)

Bitterns are among the rarest and most threatened bird species. Nearly half of the UK's bitterns live at Leighton Moss and Minsmere

rarities as marsh pea and milk parsley and several rare water weeds. Like much of the Broads system, they have suffered from water pollution in recent years, but since much of the area has been isolated from the polluted River Yare, water quality has improved along with plant diversity. The variety of plants attracts rare moths and dragonflies as well as swallowtail butterflies.

Reeds have also managed to colonise more urban areas such as Radipole Lake in the centre of Weymouth. And although certain birds do not use this site, it has proved to be an important migration point for warblers, including aquatic warblers travelling from their eastern European breeding areas. The reedbeds are also an important roost site for wagtails and hirundines.

The use birds make of reedbeds as a breeding habitat varies almost as much as the habitat itself. Birds such as mute swans, great crested grebes, pochards and coots use the reed edge to nest in, but get almost all their food from the open water and, of course, breed in many other types of aquatic vegetation. True reedbed birds have to be specialists, living in and exploiting this dense habitat, both as a feeding and nesting site. Several of these birds are rare and their rarity is mainly due to the restricted area of suitable habitat now remaining.

Bitterns are now the rarest of our breeding reedbed birds. About half of the British breeding population is at Leighton Moss and Minsmere which, along with the English Nature site at Walberswick, are the most important sites for the species in Britain.

Reed warbler

The booming call of the male, described by many observers as a foghorn or by children as someone blowing across the top of a milk bottle, has a tremendous carrying capacity. This territorial and advertising call can be heard over three miles away. RSPB research has shown that each male has an individually distinct voice, and this can be used to give an accurate count of the numbers of males present each year. Radio tracking studies at Leighton Moss have shown that the males need large areas, of up to 50 ha (124 acres), in which to breed. Bitterns nest far apart, spread over large areas of habitat that is difficult to work in, so it is one of the most difficult species to study; indeed a researcher can spend all day at a reedbed site and have only two or three fleeting glimpses of his subject! This is why techniques such as radio tracking are so useful. Bitterns feed mainly by sight and only feed in areas where water is clear and deep. Fish are their preferred diet, especially eels and sticklebacks, but they also eat amphibians, small mammals and invertebrates.

Creating new reedbeds, controlling pollution and habitat improvements are all being undertaken in a bid to reverse the decline in bittern numbers which has occurred since the 1960s.

In contrast to the bittern, bearded tits have increased and extended their range since the 1960s. At that time, bearded tits were restricted to East Anglia, with a population probably of under 10 pairs following the snowy winter of 1947. Helped by reedbeds in Holland, formed during the Zuider Zee reclamation, this species has expanded along the south coast to Radipole Lake, up the east coast to Blacktoft Sands in the early 1960s, across to Leighton Moss in 1973 and it has also recently colonised Scotland. This delightful bird is not a real tit, but is the only European member of the mainly African/Asian parrotbill family. It is well adapted to a reedbed existence,

feeding on reed seeds in winter and reedbed invertebrates during spring and summer. Birds need grit to help digest the harder reed seeds, so groups can often be seen picking up grit on the reserve paths or mud in the autumn. In most years, some birds move out of their home reedbed in autumn, and this can be the best time to see them, especially on calm sunny mornings. There is a great deal of activity, with much calling and high flying before parties move – either out to other reedbeds for the winter or at times to colonise new areas.

Bearded tit nests are tucked into the top of the reed litter, the accumulation of several years of growth and decay which forms in the lower parts of the reedbed. The densest litter occurs in the drier parts of the reedbed, so some dry areas are essential. However, many of the invertebrates on which they feed live in areas of open water. Therefore, the combination of open water, dry and wet reed are all important for this species. On RSPB nature reserves, the largest colony occurs at Blacktoft Sands, with up to 100 pairs.

Another recent success story has been the marsh harrier. In 1971, only one pair bred, at Minsmere, whereas now the total British population is in the region of 100. The reason for the spectacular increase is thought to be the withdrawal of organochlorine pesticides which decimated the populations of many birds of prey in the 1960s. It is quite usual for the male to have more than one mate, especially where the population is high, as it is on several nature reserves. Marsh harriers prey on small birds and mammals, especially rabbits and young birds. Prior to the chicks hatching, much of the adults' hunting is done over the reedbeds but, as the young grow, they regularly hunt in the surrounding countryside. The large nest is usually built well into the reedbed, with no marked preference for wet or dry areas.

Reed bunting

As the population has increased, this former summer visitor is now staying for the winter, especially in East Anglia and Humberside.

The sudden explosive squeal of the water rail has startled many a visitor. This species occupies the floor of the reedbed, its slimline body allowing it to squeeze through the thick growth at ground level. It is not exclusively confined to reedbeds, occurring also in other marshy vegetation, but it probably reaches its highest density in wet reedbeds. It is usually one of the most difficult reedbed species to see, but it occasionally appears at the reed edge, and during periods of frost it often becomes highly visible as the birds resort to the few remaining areas of open water. The water rail is found on all RSPB reedbed reserves, although only a few occur in the intertidal reedbeds of Blacktoft Sands and Titchwell. This was a difficult species to census until a new method was developed: a short snatch of a call is played on a tape recorder to which the resident water rails respond by calling back. Water rails are more abundant at several sites than previously thought.

Reed warblers are often regarded as the most typical small birds of reedbeds, but while it is true that they generally prefer reedbeds for nesting, they will breed in other drier habitats, such as willowherb. The reed warbler is one of the favourite hosts of the cuckoo; indeed at some sites studies have shown that the destruction of eggs by the cuckoo had more influence on breeding success than the food supply. For breeding, sedge warblers head for the drier areas, preferring the interface between reed and other vegetation, especially sedge, rush and willows. In late summer, both species feed throughout the marshland habitat, the reed warbler taking free-flying insects while the sedge warbler feeds on the abundant plum-reed aphid, an excellent food source which allows this Africa-bound warbler to prepare for its long migration. It quickly puts on fuel in the form of fat, in some cases almost doubling its weight in a few days before setting off to accomplish the flight in a series of long hops, refuelling at wetlands along the way. Reed and sedge warblers are migrants and breed in all RSPB reedbed reserves. Cetti's warbler is a resident, a recent colonist of Britain that first bred in 1961. It prefers the scrubby edges of reedbeds. Two other rare warblers also occur: Savi's and aquatic. The former is a rare summer visitor and has occasionally nested in some of the East Anglian nature reserves, while the latter is a late summer migrant, especially to sites such as Radipole Lake and Marazion Marsh in Cornwall.

Reed buntings are common on most reedbed reserves, although recent studies suggest they are rapidly declining, due mainly to problems when they leave the reedbeds in winter and move primarily into agricultural land. They are spread throughout the reedbed, with the highest

Otter

Hen harriers

concentrations on the drier edges as the reed merges with other habitats.

Reedbeds are not only important for breeding birds, many use them as roost sites. Most spectacular are the massed flocks of thousands of starlings, sand martins or swallows. Smaller numbers of wagtails, thrushes and buntings also roost, with hen harriers using the reedbed as a winter roost. In winter, many wrens move into reedbeds, and survive better there in a snowy winter than in woodland. Blue tits also visit reedbeds in large numbers, although numbers vary from year to year. They feed on the insects that overwinter in the reed stems.

No mammal is restricted exclusively to reedbeds, although several species make their home there. The harvest mouse is at home in a reedbed, living an aerial life among the reed stems in summer but descending to lower levels in winter. Both water shrews and water voles live a mainly aquatic life. The shrew appears still to be abundant, but water vole populations have been declining due to predation from the introduced North American mink. Surprisingly perhaps, good populations of red deer occur at both

Opposite page: common reeds at Strumpshaw Fen in Norfolk

Leighton Moss and Minsmere, lying up, browsing and even giving birth within the sanctuary of the reedbeds. Roe deer are well distributed, but are more a reed edge and scrub dweller. Otters also occur, regularly building 'couches' of dead reed just within the reed edge and lying up there during the day. The reedbed cover is important, but of course otters get almost all their food, mainly fish, from the open water areas.

Although over 700 species of invertebrates have been recorded in reed and its associated vegetation, only 40 are entirely dependent on it. The species diversity of true reedbed invertebrates may be rather poor, but many species occur in large numbers, including several species of wainscot moths. The caterpillars of some species live within the reed stem, eating off the growing point and so stopping the reed from flowering. On some nature reserves with the drier reedbeds, this can damage large areas of the reedbed. The most prolific invertebrate is the plum-reed aphid, which overwinters on *Prunus* trees before moving to reed in summer. In good years, these aphids become super abundant: warblers avidly fed on them before setting off on their long migratory journeys to Africa.

To the casual observer, the sweep of reeds in an extensive reedbed gives an appearance of unchanging permanence. However, a reedbed is but one stage in the natural vegetational succession from open water to woodland.

To maintain the habitat, and so safeguard populations of the reedbed birds described above, the RSPB manages reedbeds with the aim of slowing down or even reversing the inevitable succession to woodland.

Hen harrier

This can be done by raising the water table in at least part of the reedbed; and has been done successfully at Leighton Moss, Titchwell and Minsmere. Or there is a much more expensive option of removing, with large excavators, the accumulated organic layer, and allowing the reeds to grow in the much wetter conditions. This, along with rotational reed cutting, keeps the bed in tip-top condition.

As the reedbed ecosystem dries out, many other plants invade the reed, giving rise to a reedfen which, especially in East Anglia, can include several notable rarities. As further organic matter accumulates, woody plants can grow, leading to carr woodland of willow and alder. Both these habitats have their own species and are used at times by reedbed species. However, if this process is allowed to go unchecked, reed will disappear.

With concern mounting for reedbed species such as the bittern, the RSPB has turned to extending the area of reed, either by the creation of new reedbeds or the extension of existing sites. This exciting phase has already started at sites such as Malltraeth in Anglesey and Lakenheath in Suffolk. The return of agricultural land or old peat diggings to specially designed reedbeds is a great challenge, especially as time is crucial. Rather than wait for natural colonisation to take place, the process is being accelerated by planting reeds, either by using pot-grown plants, transplanted rhizomes or seed dispersal. The aim is to create sufficient new reedbeds and improve the existing ones so that the bittern population can increase from its present level of 20 pairs to 100 by the year 2020. The RSPB is taking the lead in this quest, but has been joined by many other organisations such as English Nature and The Wildlife Trusts.

Reedbed reserves are exciting and thrilling places. Visitors should remember though that patience is needed for this unique habitat to reveal its secrets. Those who persevere will be rewarded with unforgettable sights.

John Wilson

C H Gomersall (RSPB Images)

The swallowtail butterfly is a spectacular summer visitor to Strumpshaw Fen

Opposite page: hen harriers use reedbeds as winter roosts

Sedge warbler

It's wet underfoot

In the lowlands of Britain and Ireland, there are few habitats so rich in birds as the meadows and marshes that make up our lowland wet grassland. No-one who has heard the drumming of a snipe over a damp field on a May evening, or the whistling calls of wigeons on a cold morning in January, could fail to be captivated by the sheer diversity of birds in these wet places.

The importance of lowland wet grasslands for birds cannot be underestimated. In the summer, they are the breeding grounds for large numbers of waders, especially lapwings, redshanks and snipe. In winter, they provide refuges for up to a quarter of the UK's wildfowl.

Long ago, the RSPB recognised the importance of this now scarce and declining habitat, and today nearly a quarter of all the regularly flooded lowland wet grassland in the UK is managed within RSPB nature reserves.

A threatened habitat

Originally created thousands of years ago by the vast network of rivers meandering towards the sea, lowland wet grassland areas have undergone enormous change and decline, particularly since the Second World War.

Until a few centuries ago, rivers in the lowlands of Britain and Ireland would have overflowed their banks frequently when in spate and flooded adjacent land, enriching it with silt and creating marshes and boggy fields. Today, natural flows are constrained by sluices and banks prevent flooding. Moreover, fields in the floodplains are, in most instances, well drained in the interests of agriculture. Initially, drainage was to make the fields

A Hay (RSPB Images)

better for cattle and sheep grazing, but subsequently water tables were lowered further to allow arable crops, such as potatoes to be grown. As postwar government subsidies encouraged farmers to strive for greater yields from crops and livestock, the intensive agriculture that resulted saw massive losses and degradation of wet grassland.

In the East Anglian Fens only about 3% is left of the wet grassland that was there in the 1940s. Since the 1930s, over a third of the grazing marsh in Norfolk's Broadland has disappeared, and nearly half the coastal grazing marsh in north Kent has been lost to arable farming. In Britain as a whole, more than 40% of lowland wet grassland was lost between 1930 and the mid 1980s.

Cattle grazing and yellow iris at the Nene Washes Nature Reserve

Opposite page: a reed warbler in its favoured nesting habitat

Author

James Cadbury *joined the RSPB's staff in 1969, and is now Senior Ecologist in Reserves Ecology. He has undertaken both bird and botanical surveys at such major wet grassland reserves as the Ouse and Nene Washes and West Sedgemoor. He has been editor of* RSPB Conservation Review *since 1987.*

The few grasslands in the lowlands that remain wet are highly cherished because of the great variety of birds and other wildlife that they support. Not only are the meadows and marshes vital for wading birds and wildfowl, the ditches also support at least 190 different plant species, including frogbit and water soldier, as well as three scarce dragonfly species.

The character of the habitat is maintained by two main factors – periodic flooding which mainly occurs in winter, and summer grazing by livestock, particularly cattle. Networks of ditches not only serve as water conduits for draining (and flooding) the fields, but also provide 'wet fences' to contain these animals.

An RSPB priority habitat
In the UK, only about 150,000 ha (371,000 acres) of lowland grassland remain wet enough to support breeding waders. Much of this is concentrated in six areas in England and two in Northern Ireland. The RSPB has reserves at five of these: Mid Yare, Berney Marshes (Norfolk), Ouse and Nene Washes (Cambs), North Kent Marshes and West Sedgemoor (Somerset).

The RSPB also has nature reserves in smaller areas of wet grassland: Boyton

Marshes, Minsmere and North Warren (Suffolk), Old Hall Marshes (Essex), Pulborough Brooks (West Sussex), Exminster Marshes (Devon), Marshside (Ribble Estuary, Lancs) and Malltraeth Marsh (Anglesey). The total area of wet grassland at RSPB nature reserves is almost 5,000 ha (12,500 acres), and most of this is in a state suitable for breeding waders.

Breeding waders
The lapwing, snipe and redshank are the commonest of the eight species of wader that breed on lowland wet grassland. In the southern half of England, intensive farming has led to such low breeding success of lapwings that they have suffered a drastic population decline. Wet grasslands are among the few sites where the species can be seen breeding in anything like its former numbers. Whereas lapwings favour closely grazed pasture with scattered pools, highest densities of breeding snipe occur in damp fields on peaty soils. When moist, such substrate enables birds to probe with their long bills for earthworms and other invertebrates. Snipe nests, unlike those of lapwings, are concealed in tussocks. Although a high proportion of British redshanks breed on saltmarshes, inland they favour wet pastures with shallow pools and well-filled ditches with cattle trampled banks. They nest in shorter grass and sedge tussocks.

The Ouse Washes as a whole, when not flooded in spring, supports nearly 400 drumming snipe together with about 130 pairs each of lapwings and redshanks. On coastal grazing marsh at Elmley in Kent, there are about 170 pairs of lapwings and 100 pairs of redshanks, but because of the clay soils, only one or two drumming snipe. The RSPB's West Sedgemoor Nature Reserve, with about 50 pairs of lapwings, 25 drumming snipe and 10 pairs each of redshanks and curlews, has a major proportion of the waders breeding on the Somerset Moors and Levels.

RSPB wet grassland reserves have more than half Britain's tiny breeding population of about 40 pairs of black-tailed godwits. This handsome wader has bred at the Ouse Washes since 1952 and numbers rose to 64 pairs in 1972. In recent years, however, a spate of late spring flooding has severely disrupted the nesting godwits on the washes and the population has crashed to less than 10 pairs. However, about 14 pairs now breed regularly at the nearby Nene Washes. In early spring, the breeding birds on these two washlands are augmented by over 1,000 black-tailed godwits en route to their Icelandic breeding grounds. Elsewhere, a few breeding pairs of godwits occur on coastal grazing marshes in eastern England from the Humber to Kent.

Flocks of over 200 ruffs may occur on flooded wet grasslands in early spring, but only small numbers of males stay on late enough to attain breeding plumage and gather to display or 'lek'. Although in the 1970s and 80s, five to 21 reeves (females) may have nested at favoured sites such as the Ouse Washes, in recent years there have probably been fewer than five remaining to breed in the whole of Britain.

Crakes and quails – voices from the tall grass

Three other rare breeding birds are associated with wet grasslands at RSPB nature reserves. One is the enigmatic spotted crake which is usually detected by its far-carrying 'whiplash' call after dark between late April and June. Two or three are heard calling from stands of reed sweet-grass in the wetter areas of the Ouse Washes most years. Like the spotted crake, the quail is a summer visitor to Britain. This small gamebird is normally associated with arable fields on chalky downland, where its trisyllabic 'wet-my-lips' call indicates the presence of a male. In recent years, a small population has been returning regularly to rough grassland that is mown late at West Sedgemoor. Up until

A Hay (RSPB Images)

Mute swans nesting on the Nene Washes

the early 1900s, 'crekking' corncrakes would have been a familiar night sound from wet grasslands in southern Britain. Except in the Shannon Callows in western Ireland, this habitat has long been vacated by the corncrake as its breeding range contracted north-westwards. However, in recent years, calling corncrakes have turned up at such RSPB wet grassland reserves as the Ouse Washes and West Sedgemoor.

Breeding wildfowl

Although the mallard is the most abundant and ubiquitous breeding duck of wet grasslands, it is shovelers and garganeys which are particularly associated with this habitat. Shallow flooding in spring encourages more wintering and passage shovelers to stay and breed. So, in wet springs, the population may be several times that in drier ones. In the 1970s, there were springs in which about 300 male

Lapwing

shovelers were counted at the Ouse Washes; in recent years 30 has been more usual. Garganeys are a scarce summer visitor with a total UK breeding population of less than 125 pairs, most of which occur at wet grassland sites. The Ouse Washes is a stronghold. Both shovelers and garganeys nest in grass and sedge tussocks, but in shorter vegetation than that favoured by mallards. The ducklings, which feed largely on aquatic invertebrates, particularly insect larvae, can be found in ditches in June and July.

M Danegger (NHPA)

Redshanks forage for insects at the water's edge

Since the 1970s, the gadwall population has undergone a dramatic increase and expansion in range in lowland Britain. It is now the second most abundant breeding duck of wet grasslands. Another duck that appears to be on the increase is the pochard, with about 400 pairs in the UK. These are mainly concentrated on lakes and reservoirs with plenty of emergent and submerged vegetation. Reed-fringed, wide ditches on the coastal grazing marshes of Essex and north Kent are strongholds for breeding pochards: both Elmley and Old Hall Marshes Nature Reserves have over 20 pairs.

Wintering wildfowl

In terms of international importance, the wintering wildfowl of lowland wet grassland are far more significant than the breeding birds. The concentrations that gather on the floods are one of the finest ornithological spectacles in the UK. The wigeon is by far the most abundant wintering duck. Formerly a mainly coastal species in winter, protection from disturbance has attracted internationally important numbers (over 7,500) to some inland sites, including three RSPB nature reserves: the Ouse Washes, West Sedgemoor and Mid Yare. Elmley and several other coastal reserves have over 2,800 (1% of the UK total). The Ouse Washes as a whole regularly supports over 34,000. Wigeons are grazers, largely feeding on the leaves and grass shoots in fields that have been cropped intensively by livestock in summer. However, when disturbed, they seek water for refuge. For this reason, wigeon flocks rarely stray far from the water's edge.

Both teals and pintails are seed eaters, but while teals frequent the shallows at the edge of floods, pintails, with a greater reach when upending, can feed in water up to about 30 cm (1 ft) deep. Gadwalls pluck the shoots of aquatic plants and, in deeper water, associate with swans and diving coots to benefit from the plant material brought to the surface. Shovelers, feeding like baleen whales, use their tongue and fine comb-like lamellae on the edges of their long bills to filter planktonic crustaceans out of the water. When deeply flooded, wet grassland may attract large flocks of pochards which dive to feed on seeds and invertebrates, particularly snails.

Over 5,000 Bewick's swans, about a third of the world's population of this tundra swan subspecies that breeds in arctic Siberia, winter around the Ouse and Nene Washes in the Fens of Cambridgeshire and

Norfolk. Most of these swans feed on the surrounding arable land, where waste grain, potatoes and sugar beet tops provide abundant food. It is possible to see more than a thousand swans in one field. They fly back to the flooded washes to drink, bathe and roost at night. The floods on the Berney Marshes Nature Reserve are used by over 300 roosting Bewick's swans. Smaller numbers are now a regular sight at West Sedgemoor and Pulborough Brooks.

The whooper swans that winter in the UK are, as far as we know, virtually all from the Icelandic breeding population. Most winter in Scotland and Ireland, but numbers occurring at the Ouse Washes have now increased to about 1,000. They are attracted particularly by the grain and potatoes put out at the Wildfowl & Wetlands Trust Observatory, but they also feed on waste crops on the surrounding farmland. The Ouse Washes support one of the largest wintering concentrations of mute swans in Britain, with an average of over 600 in recent winters.

Both the European white-fronted geese and bean geese that winter in Britain occur largely on lowland wet grassland. In the 1980s, the white-fronts were concentrated largely on the Severn Estuary, but with less disturbance, increasing numbers are wintering in East Anglia and south-east England. Elmley, Mid Yare, Berney Marshes and North Warren are all RSPB nature reserves where over 100 occur. Most of the bean geese wintering in Britain belong to the western race that breeds in the forested regions of Scandinavia. They nearly all occur in two flocks, the largest (over 400) feeds at the Mid Yare Nature Reserve. They favour a longer grass sward than the closely grazed pasture frequented by wigeons and white-fronted geese.

Herons, birds of prey and owls

The rivers and ditches of lowland wet grasslands provide fish – notably eels – and frogs for grey herons. Most of the RSPB's wet grassland nature reserves have heronries in overlooking woods; the colony at Northward Hill with about 200 nests, is the largest in Britain. Wet grassland is also good for raptors: kestrels and, in winter, short-eared owls hunting for voles; a peregrine causing panic among flocks of waders and wildfowl; both marsh and hen harriers; and in late summer an agile hobby catching dragonflies in flight. These grasslands are strongholds for barn owls. Long-eared owls frequently nest in old crow and magpie nests near the Nene Washes.

M Hamblin (RSPB Images)

Passerines

The typical breeding passerines of lowland wet grassland are the sedge warbler and reed bunting where the vegetation is tall and rank, and meadow pipit and yellow wagtail where it is grazed by livestock. The male wagtails, matching buttercups for brilliance, are an unforgettable sight as they dart among the feet of cattle to snap up flies. RSPB nature reserves with good populations of yellow wagtails are Elmley and the Ouse Washes. There has, however, been a considerable contraction in the

Yellow wagtails are among the most colourful of wet grassland birds

range of yellow wagtails in Britain; it is now absent from most of the west and south-west.

Two passerines that have almost disappeared as breeding species from lowland wet grassland are the tree sparrow which nested in willows (and nestboxes) and whinchats. In late summer, large flocks of twittering goldfinches gather to feed on the seeds of thistles and teasels, while in early spring, flocks of fieldfares feed in the pastures.

Hairy dragonfly

R Thompson (NHPA)

Dragonflies
The ditches and rivers of wet grasslands are of high conservation importance for dragonflies and aquatic plants. Twenty species of dragonfly have been recorded at the Ouse Washes and 19 at West Sedgemoor. Two species that have increased in recent years and are now common where such habitat occurs in southern Britain, are the migrant hawker and ruddy darter. West Sedgemoor is a stronghold of the hairy dragonfly, one of

Meadow pipit

the earliest species to be on the wing. Several scarce dragonflies occur at RSPB nature reserves with wet grassland: the variable damselfly that is well established at both the Ouse and Nene Washes and at West Sedgemoor; the scarce emerald which is associated with well-vegetated ditches on coastal grazing marsh at Old Hall Marshes and Northward Hill; and the scarce chaser which has colonies at both the Ouse Washes and Mid Yare. The Norfolk hawker is restricted in Britain to a small area in Broadland where it is associated with ditches that still have an abundance of water soldiers, an aquatic plant. This extremely localised dragonfly occurs at the RSPB's Mid Yare Nature Reserve.

Ditch plants
There are about 190 plant species associated with ditches on grazing marshes. Fifty-three are aquatics that are wholly or largely supported in the water (such as pondweeds) or are free-floating (such as duckweeds). Then there are the emergents, such as the flowering rush, which root under water, but have leaves and flowers that project above it. In a third category are the plants which require damp conditions, but do not necessarily grow in water. Examples include purple loosestrife and water forget-me-not which occur on ditch banks.

Broadland ditches such as those on the Halvergate Marshes (not an RSPB reserve) are among the most species rich. This is to an extent due to their relatively unpolluted condition. A high proportion of lowland ditches, however, exhibit signs that they are highly eutrophic, that is enriched by nitrates and phosphates. Not only is the water opaque because of algal blooms, but the surface is frequently carpeted with floating green algae and duckweeds. Few submerged aquatics except hornwort are able to compete with such dense carpets and many thrive poorly in highly nutrient-enriched water.

The water soldier and frogbit are two floating aquatic plants that appear to be sensitive to high nutrient levels. The Broadland grazing marsh ditches, isolated from polluted rivers, are the stronghold for the water soldier in Britain, but even there the species has suffered a major decline. Frogbit is more widespread, but has also disappeared from many sites, including the Ouse Washes. It is nevertheless still locally abundant at West Sedgemoor and the Nene Washes. No fewer than 13 of the pondweeds that grow in lowland ditches have suffered a major decline. The fringed waterlily is locally abundant in the slow-flowing drains and rivers at the Ouse Washes, but outside the Fens is a rare native species.

Vegetation of the damp fields

Wet grassland fields away from the ditches tend not to be particularly interesting in botanical terms. For the most part, this is due to drainage and herbicides that have been applied unselectively. The swards tend to be composed predominantly of sedge and grass species. In summer at the Ouse Washes, reed sweetgrass extends as a waving sea of brilliant green over hundreds of hectares in the wettest zones. This grass has benefited from prolonged flooding in recent years. Where grazing is intensive, it is replaced by such soft-leaved grasses as marsh foxtail, fiorin and flote-grass, favoured by grazing wigeons. Reed canary grass is a feature of the ungrazed fields. Meadow foxtail, red fescue, meadow barley and crested dogstail are grasses characteristic of drier areas. At West Sedgemoor, there are some large areas of a local grassland community that feature marsh marigold, meadow rue and meadow thistle among other species. As well as providing nest-cover, sedges, such as brown and great pond-sedge and spike-rush, are an important source of seeds for ducks when the fields are flooded in winter. Sulphur water-dropwort, a scarce and declining umbellifer, is virtually restricted to hay meadows that are flooded in winter.

Management

The RSPB has not only allocated large resources to acquiring lowland wet grassland, but also to managing it. The habitat was created for and continues to be dependent on pastoral farming. The grassland plants are strongly influenced by hydrology and grazing pressure. On many of its wet grassland reserves, the RSPB has been attempting, with some success, to reverse the damaging effects of drainage. Hydrological control is the key to this. In winter, there may be more than enough water, but by May and June, when wildfowl and waders are breeding, levels may be low as a result of run-off and evaporation.

Keeping water at high levels in ditches using earth dams and flexipipe is one solution. Another, practised at Elmley and Northward Hill, is to store water from winter rain and run-off in a reservoir on the nature reserve for summer use. At West Sedgemoor, an area of 290 ha (715 acres) has been hydrologically isolated so that the

M Lane (Woodfall Wild Images)

The snipe has perfect camouflage for sitting motionless in dead vegetation

water level is independent of that in surrounding fields. Maintaining water in ditches to nearly brink level well into the bird breeding season helps keep peaty soils in adjacent fields damp, at least near the ditches. This keeps soil invertebrates such as earthworms near the surface and within reach of snipe and other waders. At West Sedgemoor, irrigation under the soil has been tried to extend the wetting effect out into the middle of the fields.

The flora and fauna of ditches have suffered not only from nutrient enrichment, but also from neglect. Unless they are wide and deep, they quickly silt up and become choked with emergent or overhanging vegetation. If ditches are to retain their aquatic plant diversity, they should be cleaned out about every five years, with only part being cleaned at any one time.

The composition of wet grassland plant communities and the structure of the sward are influenced by livestock grazing pressure. Cattle are preferred on RSPB marshes; they are less selective grazers than sheep, can cope with rank vegetation, and generally need less looking after. In recent years, about 5,000 cattle have grazed lowland wet grassland on RSPB nature reserves.

To avoid trampling of nests and young birds, cattle are usually not brought onto these sites until June, but even in the driest summers, grass remains available until October when the ground becomes waterlogged. Cattle grazing creates a tussocky mosaic of vegetation. Softer, more palatable grasses are grazed first, leaving the coarser species such as tufted hairgrass and sedges as tussocks. Cattle are also beneficial as they graze down vegetation on ditch banks, reducing the amount of shade over aquatic plants. Their trampling provides disturbed ground on which many less competitive annual plants of wetlands depend. Cattle dung can be a source of insect food for waders.

The RSPB now has considerable experience in restoring the conservation interest of grasslands degraded by drainage, intensive agriculture and, in some instances, neglect. At Elmley, the Nene Washes, Pulborough Brooks and West Sedgemoor, hydrological control and increased flooding have had dramatic effects on wintering, if not breeding, waterfowl. Protection from wildfowling and other disturbance has greatly increased wildfowl numbers at the Ouse Washes, Mid Yare and North Warren Nature Reserves.

Where and when should you go to experience lowland wet grasslands at RSPB nature reserves?

For spectacular numbers of wintering wildfowl, the Ouse Washes, on both the RSPB and Wildfowl and Wetland Trust (WWT) sections, is a choice site unless it is flooded deeply. The WWT observatory at Welney offers unrivalled views of all three species of swans at close quarters. Elmley, Pulborough and, after the end of the wildfowling season, the Nene Washes also provide some wonderful spectacles. West Sedgemoor in recent winters has held very large numbers of birds, but views are likely to be distant.

Frogbit is still common at West Sedgemoor and the Nene Washes, but has been lost from many polluted marshes

D Woodfall (Woodfall Wild Images)

Though numbers of wildfowl are usually at their highest in January, mid-February to early March is probably the best time to see them. There is usually still plenty of flood water, the main exodus of wintering wildfowl has yet to take place, and flocks of passage golden plovers and black-tailed godwits make an appearance. Bewick's swans may, however, already be on the move. Male ducks, in full breeding plumage, are displaying, pursuing females in wild aerial chases. Moreover, after the end of the wildfowling season (inland on 31 January), ducks become less wary. If you wish to see the bean geese at Buckenham (part of the Mid Yare Nature Reserve) a visit between mid-November and the end of January is advisable.

For breeding waders, Elmley offers many lapwings and redshanks, but to hear drumming snipe, visit the Ouse Washes early in the morning, or at dusk in calm weather. A stroll down the south bank of the Nene Washes from Eldernell is hard to beat, with black-tailed godwits and a heronry, as well as a good variety of other waterfowl. The best time for breeding waders and garganeys is late April until the end of May, by which time the growing vegetation begins to obscure the birds. The waders will be displaying then. To have a chance of hearing spotted crakes, a late evening visit (after pub-closing time) to the Ouse Washes in calm weather, in late May and early June, is recommended. You might hear 'singing' water rails and drumming snipe too after dark.

S Knell (RSPB Images)

The remarkable display of the male ruff is a highlight of the Ouse Washes

Many of the dragonflies are not on the wing until July and August, but for some of the scarcer species, such as the hairy dragonfly (late May and early June), Norfolk hawker and scarce chaser (June), earlier visits should be made. Most ditch plants are not at their prime until July and August. Ditches at Strumpshaw (part of the Mid Yare Nature Reserve) and West Sedgemoor, and the Counter Drain and Old Bedford River at the Ouse Washes have a rich variety of aquatic and emergent species. Brackish ditches have a different flora to freshwater ones; good examples can be observed at Elmley and Berney Marshes.

C. James Cadbury

Golden plover

Heart of the heath

Woodlarks are rightly famed for their mellifluous song

A Williams (RSPB Images)

Author

Bryan Pickess *was responsible for the management and administration of the RSPB's lowland heath nature reserve at Arne, in Dorset, for 30 years. He demonstrated the results of management to audiences from the UK and Europe, and assisted in raising public awareness of this threatened internationally important habitat. Bryan retired in 1996.*

To the conservationist, the term lowland heath conjures up a variety of images. It evokes large, open spaces, tracts of land with few trees but an abundance of colour, vivid yellows of spring gorse, purples and pinks of late summer and autumn heathers. Perhaps it is the little details that come to mind: the scolding call of a Dartford warbler, hidden in the gorse, or the quick, up-and-down dash of a grayling butterfly disturbed underfoot. There are mysterious elements too, including the eerie silence of dusk broken, almost unnoticed at first, by the distant churr of a nightjar.

To most people, these heathlands convey a feeling of wilderness, isolation and mystery; something of the distant past still surviving at the end of the 20th century.

In more prosaic terms, a heath is a community of low, tough plants growing on poor, acidic soils below 250 m above sea level. There are few such places now. In Europe, these lowland heathlands are concentrated mainly in a very restricted region bordering the North Sea, with small extensions north to southern Norway and south to Spain. Heathlands are mostly flat, easy to damage, easy to build on and to obliterate. In just two centuries, 90% of what we had has been lost. In the south of the UK, our remnant patches of heath represent a remarkable 20% of the world's heaths of this kind. It is a rare habitat and we have a sizeable share: we must therefore accept our responsibilities and do our utmost to conserve these lowland heaths.

Having said that, we also have to understand that this is a habitat of very recent origin – perhaps no more than 6,000 years old. The expanses of open countryside resulted from forest clearance from neolithic times, followed by repeated cropping until, in areas where the soil was poor and sandy, the nutrients were exhausted and the ground was abandoned. Once arable farming had ceased, the land was given over to livestock. Without animals biting off every shoot and sapling, the ground would have reverted to forest, but people here still eked out a living, of a sort, and continued to do so for centuries. While the better pieces of land, on the richer soils around the heaths, were farmed, the heaths were exploited in different ways. They provided heather and turves for fuel, for there were few trees. Faggots of gorse were gathered for firing the communal baking ovens in the hamlets. Young gorse was cut and chaffed for livestock feed, fern cut for bedding and old heath burned to stimulate a fresh growth of green shoots for ill-fed stock. While the animals grazed what green shoots they could from the heath, they were taken in at night and the dung in their stalls was gathered and used as manure on the lowland farms. Everything was taken from the heathland but nothing was put back.

After long periods of this exploitation, there were huge areas of heathland in southern England, far in excess of what we see today. The East Anglian heaths, Bagshot Heath in Surrey and especially the heaths of Wessex, offered landscapes that were extraordinarily desolate, empty of all signs of habitation. In Ashdown Forest in Sussex and Cannock Chase in Staffordshire, nearby iron ore deposits required vast amounts of wood for smelting and further heaths were created in a more recent wave of forest clearance.

Only with the coming of the Industrial Revolution did the people who scratched their living from heaths move away, drawn to the new towns and cities. A way of life integrated with the environment and, indeed, maintaining the habitat, began to fall apart. Heathland became neglected, quick to revert to scrubby woodland as birch and pine invaded, or it was treated simply as 'waste' land, ripe for development. So it has been seen by many people ever since.

Demand for timber stimulated the planting of great areas of heath with alien conifers. The march of the sitka spruce and Corsican pine changed the face of heathlands. Sand and gravel, locked up so conveniently close to the surface of the heaths, were mined from extensive quarries. Small villages, such as Ipswich and Bournemouth, grew into large towns, spilling out over heathland in all directions. Ever since, heaths have disappeared under the insidious spread of suburbia, as housing, roads, industrial estates and out-of-town shopping centres have grown where

previously there were nightjars and stonechats, adders and lizards.

Much of the heath that remains is fragmented. Isolated patches surrounded by housing are subject to vandalism, fly tipping and periodic fires. They are often too small to support a full range of heathland wildlife and too far from the next patch of heath for even the more mobile species to move in and out. Smooth snakes and sand lizards, let alone butterflies and beetles, are unable to cope with such change and such continued fragmentation.

At the moment, wholesale loss of heathland to development has been halted, after some bitter conservation battles in the 1980s. More difficult to counter is the simple neglect of heaths, no longer required to supply fuel, or to sustain herds of horses, sheep or cattle. Unless a heath is managed, it will become a wood. Remove the livestock, take away the gorse-cutter and soon the heathland will become a veritable tangle of birch saplings, willows in the wet patches and pines on the ridges. Fire is a management tool when used wisely and properly controlled: it can clear young trees and return the heath to heather and gorse for a few more years. But accidental fire – or deliberate fire intended to cause damage – can create havoc, with untold effects on the wildlife that is so dependent on the habitat.

The driest, freely-drained heaths are dominated by a mixture of heathers: bell heather flowering, followed by ling. The cycle of pioneer, mature and degenerate heather takes about 30–40 years on English heaths. Ideally, within a varied heathland with dry, damp, sandy and gravelly patches, all stages within the cycle should be present, forming a mosaic of habitats. Disturbance, often beside tracks and gullies, allows the brilliant yellow flowers of European gorse to flourish in spring.

Nightjar

There may also be either autumn flowering dwarf or Western gorse. South of the Thames, there are few other plants apart from mosses, lichens and occasional tufts of bristle bent, the wispy, golden grass that is such a characteristic sight and so complements the dark soil. Mosses and lichens create the lowest of covering on stable soils. Close to woodland edges, bracken takes hold on heaths that are not managed properly. Once well established, it smothers other heathland plants and radically changes the nature of the habitat.

Because trees are so few and the terrain tends to be broad and rolling, heaths are generally hot and dry. Sunshine is the necessary element for many invertebrates and there are many species that are confined to heathland habitat. Bees, wasps and ants are especially attracted to heaths and several species are found nowhere else. There are many spiders, including a large, pink species of crab spider, crouched among the flower-heads of heather, awaiting some unsuspecting prey. Around 50 species of moths feed on the heathers. Of these, few are obvious to the untrained eye, but not so the resplendent emperor moth. With its exuberant, dashing flight, it crosses the heather by day in late spring, the males seeking newly-emerged females, homing in on their powerful scent that can be detected far and wide on the heath. Fox moths are less visible, but a warm day in late winter will often cause their large, woolly caterpillars to break a long hibernation and roam about among the heather. A smaller moth, the true lover's knot, is often the most abundant moth on southern heaths in mid-summer.

There are butterflies too, on these heathland expanses. The brimstone requires alder buckthorn for its caterpillars. The first adults emerge from hibernation on a warm day in March, fluttering yellowish white in the bright spring sunshine. The grayling is a characteristic butterfly, one that settles with its wings closed, tilting towards the sun to cast the slenderest shadow. It may be a remarkable instance of camouflage in the face of any insect-eating enemy, then again, perhaps it is simply exploiting what little warmth there is by tilting over in this way. In any case, it is always hard to see until it suddenly flits up and away. The silver-studded blue is mostly restricted to lowland heaths. In East Anglia, its caterpillars feed on bell heather, while in Hampshire, Dorset and Devon they eat cross-leaved heath. The larvae are attended by two species of ant, which seek their honey-dew secretion at the same time offering the caterpillar some protection.

Emperor moth

A Newman (Woodfall Wild Images)

Reptiles are inextricably linked with heathland in the UK. All the British reptiles live on the heaths of Dorset: the widespread common lizard and grass snake, the slow worm and the beautifully-marked adder are there, but it is the colourful sand lizard and elusive smooth snake that are the rarest treasures. Sand lizards need mature heath, with patches of bare sand, but exactly what best suits the smooth snake is still uncertain.

Woodlark

Despite its warm, sunny aspect in summer, heathland is a harsh environment in winter. Consisting of little more than heather, gorse, and patches of scrub, it can be a hostile place. Consequently, nearly all the birds that nest on heaths are really summer visitors. Even the 'residents' such as the chaffinches, yellowhammers and linnets leave at the onset of colder weather, along with those longer-distance migrants from Africa, tree pipits and willow warblers. In winter, the open heath belongs solely to the streaky little meadow pipit.

If there is gorse, though, other birds come in. Most noticeable is the ubiquitous wren. But it is an up-and-down sort of life for the wren, which rises to high densities in good years but crashes down to a pitiful remnant after every harsh winter. Similarly, the stonechat is subject to periodic declines caused by bad winter weather, but this affects them while they are away, probably on the coast, for there are few present on a heath between autumn and March. In summer, stonechats are colourful and noisy inhabitants of the gorse brakes. In winter, the heath may play host to hunting hen harriers, which quarter back and forth in hope of finding a hapless meadow pipit or shrew.

There are other birds associated with heaths, of which the Dartford warbler is the one most intimately connected with the lowland heathland of southern England. Dartfords are real characters, buzzing from the depths of a gorse bush, flitting across the tops of the tall heather clumps, always diving out of sight and leading the hopeful observer a real dance. They are not shy exactly, just incredibly hard to see well. Patience is the key, and familiarity with the characteristic, buzzy, scolding note and the scratchy, rattling song which comes from the middle of a bush or, with luck, during a short, up-down aerial display flight. Here at last is the Dartford. And if you really are

C H Gomersall (RSPB Images)

Dartford warblers rely exclusively on heathland for survival

in luck, it may perch on top of a gorse twig for a few treasured moments, tail cocked, eye gleaming in its red ring, worth every bit of the effort it took to see it.

Dartford warblers are on the heaths all year and so, like wrens, they are susceptible to sudden and severe population crashes in periods of persistent snow and frost. Heavy winter snow is unusual on most heaths, but when it comes, it is all the more devastating, filling the gaps beneath the gorse, overwhelming the heather and cutting the Dartford warbler off from all hope of finding its tiny insect and spider food. In the mid-1990s, Dartford warblers were at a peak unsurpassed for 50 years: in 1995 there were more than 1,600 pairs. In the early 1960s, there were fewer than 20 pairs left in Britain, with a couple of pairs surviving at Arne, the Dorset site of the RSPB's premier heathland nature reserve. We bought Arne in 1966, knowing it to be an essential site for this warbler.

C Carver (RSPB Images)

Sand lizard

Nightjars, unlike Dartford warblers, survive elsewhere, in open woodland and on bracken-covered slopes, but are nevertheless characteristic of heaths. It is a crepuscular bird – that is, it is active at twilight, dawn and dusk, and almost never seen by day. It is a summer visitor, migrating in August and September to Africa and returning in May. It could not possibly survive the winter, and yet there is ample opportunity for it to thrive in summer. The key, of course, is the abundance of moths. They make a wonderful food source every summer.

The nightjar is a magical bird in many ways. The silence of a late evening in summer, with the sun's glow rapidly fading in the west, may suddenly be broken by a prolonged, mechanical, hollow vibration: the churring of a male nightjar singing from some unseen perch. The churr 'winds down' with a few slow, slurred notes before a sudden sharp 'clapping' of wings as the bird leaves his perch, then, perhaps, some nasal, un-birdlike calls as he flies away to feed. The nightjar makes a strange, long-winged, full-tailed shape as it turns and twists with remarkable agility,

catching moths in its huge mouth. It will often circle a bush or tree in search of moths.

Woodlarks, too, live in habitats other than heath but are, like the nightjar, most characteristic of the heathland/woodland edge, favouring areas of very short vegetation and bare sandy ground. In late winter or very early spring, the woodlark produces its song of the very finest quality. It has none of the constant, spirited flow of the skylark, instead producing a series of phrases, each of which repeat a simple note several times over, often in a descending cadence of extraordinary purity. It sings from a treetop, but the best performances come in a circling flight over a heath or clearing, the widening spirals reaching higher and higher until the final plummet, like a stone, brings it back to the ground.

Another summer visitor to the heaths is the dashing hobby – a small, elegant, long-winged falcon with 'red trousers' that has a turn of speed sufficient to catch swifts and martins, coupled with skilful agility that allows it to snatch small insects and fast-flying dragonflies from the air with its feet. It is often possible to marvel at the skill of a hobby as it accelerates towards an unseen insect, rises in a final, smooth glide, twists over for the final strike and then proceeds to eat its prey in mid-air as it circles, bending forwards to peck the food from its lowered feet. All that remains for the astonished watching human are the discarded insect wings, rotating gently earthwards.

Where there is more water on the heath, especially at the foot of a slope where water percolates through the sandy soil, the vegetation changes and the paler pink

Smooth snake

of cross-leaved heath replaces the deep purple of bell heather. Restricted to the heaths of Purbeck, Dorset, and the Lizard in Cornwall is another, very beautiful, and much rarer flower, the Dorset heath. In late summer and autumn, it produces elongated clusters of large, deep pink flowers. In wetter sites, purple moor grass increases, creating purple-flowered tussocks up to 75 cm high. On open spaces in grazed areas, appear diminutive plants, such as yellow centaury (very rare outside the New Forest), chaffweed and allseed. Most noticeable in summer is the heath spotted orchid, sometimes growing in profusion, while the marsh gentian is a real gem, now much diminished. Its large, bright blue trumpets point skyward in the autumn sunshine.

In really waterlogged spots, lawns of sphagnum moss become dominant. These are soft, spongy masses; dangerous places for unwary walkers. Within them, the only shrubby plant is bog myrtle, which in April produces bright ginger flowers before the leaves and has a strong, pleasant scent. In spring, the dainty, pale blue or pink flowers of heath milkwort appear, nestling in the low vegetation. In July, bright orange and yellow spikes of bog asphodel enliven the mires, sometimes in profusion. White-beaked sedge often accompanies them. Close examination of the wet ground reveals other gems, including some carnivorous plants which supplement their nutrients by trapping tiny flies and digesting their juices. These include three species of sundews, which have green and red leaves in flat rosettes,

each leaf covered in tiny, sparkling dewdrops on sticky hairs and each rosette eventually producing a thin, upstanding stem with a cluster of tiny white flowers. Pale butterwort has a different tack, so to speak, using sticky, pale green leaves, spread out like a limp starfish, which roll inwards at the edges to trap unwary creatures.

Cotton grass grows through the sphagnum where the ground is permanently waterlogged, creating thick clumps with clusters of white, cottony flowers. Boggy pools may be covered with bog pondweed and delicately-flowered bogbean, while yellow-flowered bog St John's wort graces the margins.

The mysterious churring call of the nightjar can be heard on still summer nights

M Grey (NHPA)

Such pools are magnets for wildlife. Roe deer come to drink while many birds arrive to drink and bathe. The water is acid, but many invertebrates are adapted to live with that: pondskaters and whirligig beetles among them. They may have to survive the deadly intent of the huge raft spider which will dash across the surface film of the water in pursuit of insect prey.

Perhaps the most important group is the dragonflies and damselflies. Many of them breed on lowland heath pools and several are almost restricted to them. Yet, like other threatened species of the heaths, where conditions are right they may be abundant. Male dragonflies stake out territories, in much the same way as birds. Most eye-catching are the blue and black emperor dragonflies, which emerge in late spring. Streams are preferred by golden-ringed dragonflies while bog pools attract large red damselflies and scarce small red damselflies.

Opposite page: linnet on gorse

There is always something to see on a heath. What may, at first glance, look rather bare and bleak becomes rich and fascinating on closer acquaintance. Above all, many of the wild creatures and plants found here are nationally rare and utterly depend on the heath for their existence. If we are to ensure a future for them, we must maintain the heathland habitat.

The RSPB has been involved with lowland heaths for several decades. It was not until the establishment of Arne Nature Reserve, in 1966, that the first real steps were taken to manage the habitat, at a time when it was rapidly disappearing. It became clear that other people – landowners, county planners and eventually European Union officials – had to be persuaded that heathland was important and threatened, and in need of urgent action. We have come a long way since then.

Hobby

While it was rightly viewed as a disaster at the time, it was the long, dry summer of 1976 and its series of rampaging heathland fires that brought the plight of our heaths sharply into focus. Daily news bulletins showed blackened gorse and the sad, charred remains of burned smooth snakes. This was a turning point for the recognition of this rapidly disappearing heritage, by the public and conservationists alike. The need to conserve heathland was recognised and at last action began to be taken. The RSPB was at the forefront of heathland protection and remains so, involved in heathland management at an increasing number of nature reserves: we now manage six large areas of heath, from Suffolk (Minsmere and North Warren) to the South Devon Pebblebeds (Aylesbeare Common) and the famous Purbeck heaths in Dorset (Arne, Grange and Stoborough).

Roe deer

Managing these heaths is expensive. At Arne alone, we have spent some £100,000 on machinery, including tractors, a forage harvester, a wood-chipper, silage trailers, and a tractor-mounted rotary brush and 'vacuum cleaner', all necessary to the management of gorse and heather and the constant battle against invading Scots pines. Even so, much management work is of a kind that has to be carried out by hand – not only is it expensive, but it is time-consuming and hard work.

Most heathland areas, especially those that are not nature reserves, suffer from the entirely natural process of invasion by trees and an inexorable return to forest. The longer this is allowed to continue, the more difficult and more expensive it is to reverse the process.

In Dorset, more than 95% of the remaining heath is designated as Sites of Special Scientific Interest (SSSIs) but, while this may help prevent destruction, it does nothing to help management and even the best heaths may be neglected. In 1988, the RSPB, well aware of this problem, drew up an ambitious plan to address it. Experience at its own nature reserves enabled the RSPB to assess the potential elsewhere and to judge the costs involved. It quickly became clear that a long-term sponsor was required. In 1989, BP generously offered to pay some of the costs over three years and the 'Dorset Heathland Project' began.

More recently, we have twice been successful in obtaining generous funding

Male stonechats find a suitable perch for singing

from the European Union which has met half of the costs of specific projects: the second package also involves heaths in Cornwall and Brittany. More than £2 million will be spent over eight years in Dorset, restoring the heaths to their former glory, complete with a full complement of sand lizards, smooth snakes, silver-studded blues, marsh gentians and Dartford warblers. Government schemes, including the Countryside Stewardship, Reserve Enhancement and Wildlife Enhancement schemes, now allow the reintroduction of ponies, cattle and sheep onto heaths.

The momentum begun by the RSPB's initiative is continuing, but constant pressure is essential. If the heaths are neglected again, their wonderful wildlife and landscapes will revert to scrub and ultimate oblivion.

Heath fritillary

Opposite page: bell heather and purple moor grass on a Surrey heath

Lowland woodland

The eerie quietness in the frosty stillness of a winter's wood; the exuberance of spring when the woodland is decked in blue, white and yellow flowers and the morning air is brimming with birdsong; the mellow, sultry charms of a walk in its cool sanctuary in summer or, most poignant of all, the yellowing trees in autumn, leaves tumbling out of the sky. Such sensations are so familiar to millions of people as to scarcely need description. Yet, because it is such a commonplace, the local wood is too often taken for granted. We do not stop to think whether our grandchildren will be able to show their children the same bluebell dell or the hideaway in the hollow bole of that massive beech. Nor does it occur to us that the wood, perhaps now disfigured by supermarket trolleys and mattresses, has a fascinating story to tell, of its origins, past management and present threats.

When Britain's ice cover melted away after the last glaciation some 10,000 years ago, a gaunt, treeless landscape was exposed. Lowland Britain, which includes most of England apart from the Pennines, escaped the worst ravages, but even those favoured southern counties which were never covered with ice were too cold to support tree growth. So our present lowland woods are relatively young. The natural lifespan of an oak is three or four hundred years, so the woodlands' interdependent communities of birds and insects, plants and mammals have evolved in the course of a mere 25 or so oak generations.

As the climate gradually improved, the harsh landscape was soon softened by vegetation and it was not long before the first trees – pines and birches – re-established themselves. No remnant of those early pinewoods remains in the

S Knell (RSPB Images)

Willow tit

Opposite page: beech wood

lowland region. As the climate continued to change, now warmer, now wetter, the pioneer birches and pines were replaced by other species, and there is no reason to suppose that woodland is not still subtly adapting to long-term meteorological trends. Global warming could change our woods beyond recognition, with shallow-rooted trees like beech dying out altogether.

It has been suggested that the natural tree cover in Britain is oakwood, but this is probably an over-simplification and it is more likely that, prior to human intervention, the woods were a mosaic of different species. Even today, it is obvious to a casual observer that all woods are not the same. It may be that one wood is a haze of bluebells when another shimmers

Author

Michael Walter *graduated from Durham University in zoology and botany in 1970. Over the past 15 years, as RSPB warden at Blean Woods, Canterbury, his particular interest has been the creation of wildlife-rich habitats out of sweet chestnut coppice.*

with wood anemones: wellington boots may be essential all year round in one wood, yet in a nearby copse it may be possible to walk dry-shod in most months. There may be a dramatic difference in the species of woodland trees between one wood and the next.

An ancient beech wood in the New Forest

D Woodfall (Woodfall Wild Images)

Although the mixture of trees in a wood can be very varied, it is often possible to pick out different types of woodland. For example, on low-lying, waterlogged soil, alder and willow will tend to predominate and, in the days before drainage work was undertaken, this sort of woodland would have been much more extensive. Here woodcocks can probe deeply for worms, mallards and moorhens nest, and the soft wood of mouldering alder trees provides an ideal site for the willow tit to excavate a nest-hole. Enriched with minerals washed in by floods or springs, the soil supports a lush growth of plants: hazel, guelder rose and other shrubs flourish here, providing plenty of cover for species like the blackcap, wren, dunnock and nightingale. Above, in the tree canopy, siskins, redpolls

Woodcock

and goldfinches feed on the seeds trapped in the little cone-like alder fruits.

On nearby, slightly higher ground the soil is better drained, but still enriched by occasional floods. Here you may find ashwoods, beneath whose light shade hazel and other shrubs can thrive, providing habitat for many woodland birds. Ash seeds are taken by bullfinches and hawfinches.

Few trees do really well on infertile or dry soils and here woods are likely to be dominated by birch, beech or oak. The heavy shade of beech, which is usually the principal tree on chalk downs, tends to suppress plant growth and consequently restricts the variety of birds, but the crop of beech mast is a favourite with great tits and winter-visiting bramblings. If the soil is very infertile, the woodland may have an open, heathy character, and on such ground birch is often the only coloniser, although scattered oaks may later grow up in the shelter of the birches. These woods have some of the characteristics of upland woods, so it is not surprising that redstarts, wood warblers and tree pipits occur in the oakwoods growing on poor soil at Blean Woods, the RSPB woodland reserve in Kent. Birches produce vast quantities of tiny seeds, which are relished by redpolls. Here too, blue tits revel in their acrobatic prowess, swinging upside down from the delicate twigs in order to reach insects lurking in the catkins or buds, while their heavier cousins, the great tits, must content themselves with a less athletic search among sturdier branches or else on the ground, attacking nuts with their stout bills.

On soils ranging from damp clay to fertile loam, other trees may be dominant in different woods – elm in parts of Northward Hill in Kent, aspen at Wolves Wood in Suffolk, and hornbeam at Fore Wood, Sussex, for example. Hornbeam is often found covering large areas of southern woodland to the exclusion of other trees, and its very dense shade excludes most other vegetation, giving such woods a resemblance to the clean-floored beech woods. Its small, hard seeds are a particular favourite with hawfinches and greenfinches.

This very general account of some of the trees to be found in lowland woods shows that certain birds tend to be associated with particular trees but, additionally, the presence or absence of a good shrub layer can be crucial in determining whether or not certain birds will occur in a wood. In fact, it is the general structure of a wood rather than its tree species which determines what birds will be present. Old trees are important to many hole-nesting birds, so on RSPB nature reserves individual trees or whole blocks of the wood are left to die on their feet in order to ensure a plentiful supply of nest-holes. By contrast, in commercially managed woods, trees are usually felled before they are old enough to have developed natural holes, so species such as tits and nuthatches may be fairly scarce even though there is an abundance of food. A wood with an uninterrupted tree canopy will support a less interesting range of birds than one which is broken up by clearings or glades where dense undergrowth can become established, enabling species such as garden warblers and whitethroats to breed.

The whitethroat barely qualifies for inclusion in the category of woodland species, being very much a bird of young scrub. It must have been quite rare when lowland Britain was covered in woods, but today's landscape with hedges, copses and tangled margins of countless small woods, provides plenty of scope for colonisation by this warbler. However, this pattern of fragmented woodland is not suitable for some larger species such as honey buzzards and goshawks, birds which must

have been far commoner in the ancient, extensive woods. Another factor which should not be forgotten is geographical location: nightingales will not be heard in apparently ideal woodland habitat in the Midlands, for they are at the northern edge of their breeding range in southern England; and we will listen in vain for the stentorian drilling of woodpeckers or the mysterious hooting of tawny owls in Ireland.

A wood is a private, self-contained world. On entering one, you are enfolded by its trees, their foliage filtering out the tiresome noise of human activity. On a windy day, the wood will seem a sheltered haven; during drought there will still be damp places; in hot weather it will be deliciously cool in the heavy shade; and in the depths of winter, frosts are less likely to penetrate. Birds are not slow to appreciate the advantage of this more equable climate. When exposed fields and marshes are baked hard in summer or frozen solid in winter, birds like woodcocks, redwings and blackbirds will be drawn to the woods.

E A Janes (NHPA)

Bluebell woods are a phenomenon unique to the British Isles

Relatively few birds spend their entire lives within the wood's confines: among these might be listed the treecreeper, lesser spotted woodpecker and tawny owl. Many more species, such as tits, robins and great spotted woodpeckers, often spend part of the winter foraging further afield in hedgerows and gardens. The reason for this ebb and flow of birds is bound up with the availability of food. Insect breeding ceases in the winter months, so predation by birds gradually depletes the stock of food, whereas the advent of warmer spring weather initiates a rapid increase in insect numbers, the most conspicuous manifestation of which is the abundance of defoliating caterpillars in the trees in late May and June. At this time, seed-eating species abandon their specialised diet in favour of the easy pickings, which are fed to their nestlings. It is this seasonal abundance of food that enables woods to support not only the resident birds but also the summer visitors such as warblers, spotted flycatchers and cuckoos. During this period of plenty, house sparrows and crows, which are not normally associated with woodland, may venture in to claim their share of the spoils. While all these species feed in woods to a certain extent, herons and rooks are exceptional, nesting in woods but feeding exclusively in open land.

To appreciate how woods gained their present form, it is necessary to know something of the human influence on them in the past 5,000 years or more. Ever since

people returned to these islands after the last glaciation, we have been modifying the woodland cover, initially by creating small clearings in which to practise primitive farming, latterly by managing the remaining woodland as a source of material for multifarious domestic, agricultural and industrial requirements. Even by Saxon times, so much woodland had been destroyed that some parishes were short of wood and it may have been then that people began to conserve this precious resource. One way of doing this is by coppicing. The cut stumps of trees send up a fresh crop of shoots, or coppice. In their competition for light, the shoots grow up quickly into thin poles which, after as little as 10 years' growth, are sturdy enough to be put to a variety of uses. Medieval woodcutters could crop the trees' coppice growth indefinitely, so there was no need to replant, and the only extra work involved some form of fencing or ditching to safeguard the young, palatable shoots from the attentions of deer or livestock.

Most lowland woods have been managed as coppice for hundreds of years, though a scattering of oak trees was often retained for felling at longer intervals to satisfy the demand for the larger timber needed in buildings and boats. These coppices, cut fairly regularly, were therefore in a permanently young state, with an abundance of shrubby growth for at least half of the cycle. But the practice fell into decline early in the 20th century and today most of these woods, formerly providing employment for thousands of woodcutters and their felling-axes, stand derelict – too old to form workable coppice, yet too young to have developed into mature, diversified woodland.

Such woods tend to be rather dull, heavily shaded and poor in bird life. Fore Wood was in just such a state when it was bought by the RSPB in 1976. It supported a fair number of species, like treecreepers and

The song of the nightingale can be heard in a number of southern woodland reserves

A Hay (RSPB Images)

D Woodfall (Woodfall Wild Images)

Sessile oakwood in Dyfed

dazzling array of flowers appears – primroses, violets, orchids, wood anemones, bluebells and others, their dormant seed or buried rootstock suddenly prodded into life by the sunlight flooding the earth for the first time in 15 years or more. Butterflies, too, quickly colonise the sun-drenched clearings in a profusion of colourful fluttering. After two or three years, the growth of more aggressive plants like bramble chokes out the delicate spring flowers, but subsequent coppice growth gradually shades out the brambles, so that by the time the area is cut again the ground is fairly bare and ready for the flowers. This regular management can also bring financial rewards: at Blean, Tudeley and Stour Woods, the annual coppicing programme generates thousands of pounds of income from the sale of wood for charcoal, firewood, woodchips, fencing, hedging stakes, beams, planks and furniture.

The even rhythm of coppicing and regrowth conjures up an image of an unruffled, unchanging rural craft, but humans must long ago have found themselves dissatisfied with the often crooked poles that would become brittle with rot within a year of harvesting. The problem was overcome by planting coppice that better suited their purposes. Sweet chestnut, a native of southern Europe, can grow into a fine, massive-boled tree, but when treated as coppice, it sends up a cluster of straight poles which are remarkably resistant to decay. In recent centuries, in the warmer counties of southern England, thousands of acres of native coppice have been replanted with this alien tree. Unfortunately, it lacks the wealth of insect life associated with many indigenous trees, so chestnut coppices are rather barren areas, their sterility emphasised by the way birds are drawn to any oaks which may be present. Extensive areas of Blean Woods were dominated by chestnut coppice, but much of it has been

tits, but held few wrens or warblers, which need a certain amount of bushy cover. Management there since 1978 has concentrated on opening up the wood by creating glades and rides, by thinning and coppicing. Many birds soon benefited – two pairs of willow warblers bred for the first time in 1980, 11 pairs in 1981 and 22 in 1982. Carried out up and down the country, such simple management could revitalise the thousands of abandoned coppices, large and small. Indeed, natural management on a gigantic scale occurred in southern counties in October 1987 when the 'Great Storm' felled literally millions of trees in the space of a few hours. Where there was formerly a very uniform structure, many of these 'devastated' woods were opened up overnight, becoming far more valuable to birds, with numerous warblers nesting in the scrub that has sprung up in the freshly created clearings.

Birds are by no means the sole beneficiaries of all this work. Following coppicing, a

Spotted flycatcher

swept away by recent management, to be replaced by heathland and glades.

A longer-term project involves killing some of the chestnut stumps and planting native trees to encourage an eventual reversion to oak and hazel woodland.

So natural woodland was converted to native coppice and then to deciduous plantations; now a further step has been taken in fundamentally altering woods – the planting of exotic conifers. These fast-growing trees are readily converted into accurately-machined planks which suit modern requirements better than the imprecisely straight, thin coppice poles. Huge areas of lowland coppice have been grubbed up and replaced by spruce from North America, pine from Corsica and larch from Japan – their dark, spiky profiles contrasting starkly with the undulating lowland scenery. Once the canopy has closed in, the number and variety of birds choosing to stay in the perpetual gloom plummets, and little can thrive apart from fungi. Gone are the spring flowers, the small mammals, warblers and butterflies that make deciduous woodland such a joy. Even if deciduous trees are replanted once the conifers have been felled (as is being done on our nature reserves at Arne and Blean), it will be many centuries before all the specialised flora and fauna can recolonise.

There are other threats to our remaining woodland. Least worrying is neglect – an abandoned coppice will, over the years, mature and its wildlife value increase without any intervention from people. Nor is disease likely to prove a serious problem. At Northward Hill all the elms were killed by Dutch elm disease, forcing the large heronry to shift into the nearby oaks; but now fresh shoots are springing from the still-healthy tree roots and elm woodland will eventually heal the scars.

Of more concern is the destruction of woodland to make way for new roads, housing estates and factories. Since this development usually occurs on the periphery of towns, the lost woods are the ones most valued by local people for recreation. But the area lost in this way is small by comparison with the acreages grubbed out each year up until the 1980s by farmers eager to gain a little extra land. This process is as old as farming itself, for by 1086 as much as 85% of our woodland had been cleared for agriculture. In the succeeding 900 years, half of the medieval remnant has been lost, much of it this century, and yet still we were hungry for land. Naturally, earlier farmers reclaimed the more fertile and better-drained land centuries ago, so today's woodland generally stands on barren or waterlogged ground which will produce indifferent pasture, and then only after the farmer has extensively drained the land, a process which, along with grubbing out, was encouraged by Ministry of Agriculture grants.

Faced with such overwhelming threats, what safeguards were there for woods? Very few, alas: the usual planning controls did not apply to those wishing to alter our countryside radically by ripping out age-old deciduous woodland. The only safeguard lay with Tree Preservation Orders, but the local council imposing such an order on a tree or wood had to be prepared to pay the owner compensation, and in times of austerity there is an understandable reluctance on the part of councils to invoke this power. Thankfully though, just such an order in 1972 prevented Wolves Wood from becoming a 90-acre barley field prior to its purchase by the RSPB.

Since about 1980, however, there has been a remarkable shift in attitude to our woodland heritage. Changes in government policy mean that conifer planting on the site of native woodland has all but ceased; and the advent of surplus farmland and the fairytale world of set-aside have eliminated the urge to convert woodland to arable. Instead, some farmers are actually planting trees on unwanted land, and there are numerous government schemes to promote this. One such initiative, the Woodland Grant Scheme, makes funds available not just for tree planting but also for managing open areas within woods and providing visitor access. Many RSPB nature reserves have been able to benefit from this grant scheme. On a grander scale, we now have government-sponsored schemes for the creation of a national forest of 40,000 ha (100,000 acres) in the Midlands and 20 or more smaller community forests on derelict, blighted land on town outskirts.

Nature is, in any case, very resilient, and will fight back, given a chance. In times of agricultural depression, abandoned farmland soon tumbles down to scrub or woodland as seedlings invade the ungrazed, untilled soil. One-fifth of the wood at Northward Hill was farmland before the First World War: the neglected fields were soon invaded by hawthorn, and recent management has turned this area into a haven for wildlife. Having lost its links with the primeval woodland, this secondary woodland cannot be expected to harbour the same wealth of animals and plants, but it is still a great improvement on a featureless field. All our woods are also

J Buckingham (NHPA)

The hawfinch is a rare and elusive woodland species, often revealed by its loud 'ticking' call

important as landscape features in their own right – Stour and Wolves Woods are oases of wildlife interest in otherwise intensively farmed landscapes. From Elmley, our wetland nature reserve on the Isle of Sheppey, Blean Woods rears up on the grey horizon as an impressively massive, brooding dome of woodland.

The future for lowland woodland looks brighter now than for many years, but our vigilance is still needed to prevent any further piecemeal nibbling away of what little remains. Primary woodland, which has supported tree growth ever since the recolonisation of these islands by trees, is a living link with our past, a priceless heritage to be treasured, not squandered. When 93% of the lowlands are mainly devoted to agriculture, housing and industry, is it really too much to ask that a mere 7% should be kept as woodland where future generations may thrill to the rich tones of the nightingale or gaze in wonder on a seemingly endless carpet of bluebells?

The wooded hills

Stream through a Perthshire woodland

N Benvie (RSPB Images)

One of the most evocative sounds of spring must be the soft accelerating trill of the wood warbler. Set against a sunlit canopy of fresh yellowish-green oak leaves and a woodland floor of bluebells and primroses, spring in a western oakwood is a wonderful experience. With a whole range of other birds bursting into song, as well as flowers in profusion, there is an air of anticipation as another season gets underway.

The distribution of breeding wood warblers very neatly reflects the main areas of upland woodland in Britain. The wood warbler has a firm westerly bias, with strongholds in Devon and Cornwall, Wales and the Marches, parts of the Lake District, west Scotland and the Great Glen. It is also in these regions that some of the best upland oakwoods can be found, often

intermixed with other hardwood species. Further north into Scotland, Scots pine features in some areas, while in the far north of Britain, our upland woodlands are dominated by birch.

Sadly, these native woodlands today are a poor reminder of the great forests which once dominated much of Britain. By Roman times, clearing for agriculture was well underway and the forest became increasingly fragmented. This pattern of clearances continued throughout the Norman period, despite the fact that the nobility set aside some of the best remnants as royal hunting forests.

As early as Medieval times, it was realised that something had to be done to slow down this rapid depletion of resources. As a result, the system known as coppicing came into widespread operation. The earliest evidence of coppicing management dates back to Neolithic times, somewhere between 2200 and 2500 BC. By the time the Domesday Book was written in 1086, the system was practised throughout lowland England and into Devon and Cornwall. During the Middle Ages, it extended across much of Wales and southern Scotland, reaching well into Argyllshire and Perthshire. Together with a growing demand for timber for iron ore smelting and major construction tasks such as house building and boat building, there was intense pressure on surviving woodlands. This pressure has never relaxed since, despite the decline of coppicing in the 19th and 20th centuries. Two world wars and the heavy grazing of the uplands by both deer and sheep have continued to decimate the surviving forest.

Today there is very little left of our native woodlands. In England, it amounts to just

Author

Mike Trubridge *first worked for the RSPB as a contract warden in 1975, and joined the full-time staff in 1981. He has worked on many RSPB nature reserves, including five years at Minsmere and eight years at Inversnaid. He is now based near Stirling in Central Scotland.*

4% of the country, while only about 3% of Wales is covered by deciduous woodland. The situation is no better in the north, where native woodlands now account for just 1% of Scotland's land area. All these few remaining areas of woodland are 'semi-natural'. There is no such thing as a natural wood anywhere in Britain: all have been interfered with in the past either by people or by their animals.

In Wales, some of the most characteristic woods are the 'hanging' oakwoods of steep, valley-side slopes. One bird above all others epitomises these woodlands of remote valleys – the red kite. Once a familiar raptor throughout much of Britain and a common scavenger in Elizabethan London, this spectacular bird was brought to the verge of extinction by the beginning of the 20th century. Persecution down the centuries reduced the kites' population to about half a dozen birds in central Wales. Since then, careful protection has helped its numbers to increase, albeit very slowly at times, and there are now more than 120 pairs in the Principality. More recently, reintroduced birds in England and Scotland have bred successfully and the future of this exciting raptor is assured.

The red kite is a magnificent flyer, circling tirelessly for hours over wooded valleys and open moorland, searching for carrion and small mammals. It nests in trees, choosing a tall oak or occasionally a larch or pine, sometimes taking over an old crow's nest. Many people visit Wales specially to see this bird and in recent years their quest has been made much easier by an imaginative scheme called 'Kite Country'. Closed circuit TV cameras overlooking a kite nest beam back live pictures to nearby visitor centres. Other birds such as buzzards, goshawks and kestrels are also filmed in this way, providing people with superb views during the breeding season.

Another bird strongly associated with Welsh oakwoods is the pied flycatcher. Unlike the resident red kite, the pied flycatcher is a summer visitor only. It arrives in April along with other trans-Saharan migrants to breed in these upland deciduous woods, before returning in August. Recent research at the RSPB's nature reserve at the Gwenffrwd in mid-Wales has helped us to determine oakwood management which would ensure the long-term survival of the woods and meet the habitat requirements of the pied flycatcher.

The Gwenffrwd is one of seven woodland nature reserves that the RSPB now manages in Wales, and it is here that an exciting project is well underway to expand this habitat. In 1989, to celebrate the RSPB's centenary, plans were drawn up to create a Centenary Wood. Forty hectares (100 acres) of bracken-covered hillside have been planted with 68,000 oak seedlings to link up scattered fragments of the original woodland cover. Today, there are no surviving large areas of deciduous woodland in Wales, just a series of dispersed remnants. These have persisted partly because they are uneconomic to clear for agriculture and partly because they have some value as shelter for stock in winter. This exciting new scheme at the Gwenffrwd will create a sizeable area of oak woodland, although it will be a long time before the woodland becomes suitable for red kites, pied flycatchers and other woodland birds.

One of the main threats to the hanging oakwoods of Wales is the high numbers of sheep. In summer, they are out on the open hills, but with colder weather in the autumn, the sheep move down from the high ground to the shelter and better grazing in the woods. Any tree seedlings are quickly nibbled, preventing the woodland from regenerating naturally. Unless extensive fencing is erected, the woods slowly die off.

Red kite

At least the Welsh woodlands do not have the additional problem of heavy grazing by deer. In the past, both red and roe deer were widespread in Wales, but by the 17th century, the red deer became extinct there, shortly followed by the roe deer. This was caused by a combination of over-hunting for venison and over-persecution as farm pests. Farther north, however, high numbers of red deer are a major problem for native woodlands.

The turkey-sized capercaillie is restricted to Caledonian pinewoods

Scotland has a greater range of upland woodland habitat than either England or Wales, but once again this habitat is under severe threat. With native woodlands accounting for only 1% of Scotland's land cover, this country has the dubious distinction of having a lower proportion of tree cover than any other European country, except for Iceland. Nevertheless, these relics are extremely important for wildlife and support some unique species.

The Scottish oakwoods are mainly located in the west and south of the country – in parts of Argyll, the Loch Lomond area and Dumfries and Galloway. In many respects they are similar to the oakwoods of Wales, although there are some subtle differences. For instance, the history of these northern woods follows much the same sequence of events as in the south, but with significant variations in timing and emphasis. Thus we find that coppicing only started in the Loch Lomond woods at the beginning of the 18th century, considerably later than in the south.

Generally speaking, the further north and west you go in Britain, the wetter the climate becomes and this, too, leads to important differences in woodland habitats. Devon and Cornwall have up to 180 days a year with rainfall, Wales has up to 220 days, while parts of western Scotland can experience 300 days of wetness annually. This moist oceanic climate is ideal for mosses and liverworts,

Scottish crossbill

collectively known as bryophytes, and as a result Scottish woods have some excellent examples of these communities. Likewise, the relatively clean air of the north-west means that lichens are prolific. There are a number of sites in Scotland which are internationally important for their extremely rich bryophyte and lichen floras.

D Tipling (RSPB Images)

But it is not only the non-flowering plants that are well represented – flowers are both numerous and varied. Walk into any deciduous woodland in spring and it is a wealth of colour and scents. One of the first flowers to appear is the lesser celandine, a member of the buttercup family. Another early flowerer is the opposite-leaved golden saxifrage, a plant of woodland flushes and stream sides, with delicate greenish flowers. But the real highlight of these spring flowers must be the bluebell. It is widely distributed and common throughout most of Britain, and bluebell woods are among the most distinctly British of all plant communities.

A visit to a bluebell wood in spring is one of nature's wonderful experiences. After a long day of warm sunshine in May, the woods are heavy with the delicate scent of myriads of bluebells. The late evening sun casts playful shadows through the tree canopy, while the woodland birds proclaim their territories for one last time. Together with other woodland favourites such as the primrose, wood anenome and wood sorrel, the bluebell is an indicator of old, established woodlands. And that is precisely what many of our upland woods are – they are quite literally hundreds of years old.

What's more, these four plants sometimes show where trees used to grow. In parts of the western Highlands, there are extensive patches of these flowers on the open moorland, well away from the present tree cover. Deprived of annual enrichment of the soil from leaf litter, they have managed to survive on the impoverished moorland by associating with bracken. Just like the leaves of a tree, the bracken fronds die back and rot down during the winter, fertilising the ground.

The bird life of these Scottish oakwoods is very similar to that of their Welsh counterparts. Summer visitors such as the pied flycatcher, redstart, tree pipit, willow warbler and wood warbler abound. Both great spotted woodpeckers and buzzards are well represented, while goosanders can be found where there are lochs and rivers nearby. Some people might not associate this duck with woodlands, but it nests in holes in trees and can sometimes be found breeding well inside a wood. Winter can often be a bleak period for woodland birdwatchers; even supposedly common birds like the song thrush will often move out to towns and villages when the weather deteriorates. However, an apparently birdless tree canopy can suddenly become full of activity when a roving party of tits moves through. Other species such as the treecreeper and chaffinch often join these groups and for a short time there are birds everywhere.

One of the more exciting mammals that is making a welcome come-back in Scotland is the pine marten. Until the early 1980s, this delightful member of the mustelid family was mainly confined to the far north-west of the country. However, following protection in the 1981 Wildlife and Countryside Act, it has quickly spread back to many of its former areas and is now fairly widespread throughout much of the country north of the Central Lowlands. By 1989, pine martens had recolonised the oakwoods of Loch Lomond, after an absence of 157 years.

The RSPB has a number of important deciduous woodland nature reserves in Scotland. In the south-west, the Wood of Cree is an excellent example of former oak coppice. Farther north on the banks of Loch Lomond, Inversnaid includes both oak woodland and the remains of the largest alder wood in Central Scotland. Killiecrankie is perhaps best known for its base-rich flushes, bryophytes and a superb range of flora, while over in the extreme west, Glenborrodale on the Ardnamurchan peninsula is a classic example of an oceanic western oakwood.

At all of these sites, visitor facilities ensure that people can enjoy the wildlife and scenery of the reserves. Generally speaking, woods are not suitable locations for birdwatching hides, but carefully designed nature trails take visitors through the best areas. In addition, panoramic viewpoints provide superb vistas of the surrounding countryside.

Unfortunately, there is one kind of wildlife in these northern woodlands that is not welcomed by visitors. This is the diminutive midge, without doubt the most talked about insect in Scotland. There are in fact 34 species of biting midge in the country, but only four or five attack humans. During the summer, this tiny insect has been known to drive people close to insanity. The bite from one midge is negligible and can pass

Pine marten

N Benvie (RSPB Images)

Scots pinewood is home to many rare species

few remnants of the Great Wood of Caledon. These are areas of Scots pine, associated with birch, which were once the dominant woodland type in the early Caledonian forest. Originally covering 1,500,000 ha (almost four million acres), the pine forest has suffered tremendous losses during the last 6,000 years and today a mere 16,000 ha (40,000 acres) are left. Some of this damage was only done very recently, for instance between 1957 and 1987 clear felling and underplanting with exotic conifers resulted in the loss of a further 25% of the remaining forest.

These native pinewoods of Scotland have the most distinctive bird community of any woodland type in Britain. This includes the crested tit, capercaillie and Britain's only endemic species, the Scottish crossbill. With other notable species like the osprey, golden eagle, black grouse and greenshank breeding in it, Caledonian pine forest must be one of our most exciting woodland habitats.

unnoticed, but when attacked by scores of these insects, life becomes unbearable. Nevertheless, this huge biomass of potential food is welcomed by the wildlife of the area and is a vital source of food for birds, mammals and plants. Species as diverse as the pied flycatcher, pipistrelle bat and common sundew thrive on these minute insects.

Grazing by both sheep and deer is one of the main problems affecting the future of many woodlands both on and off nature reserves. High levels of grazing and browsing by animals will prevent the trees regenerating. Careful control of deer by annual culls and sheep by the erection of fences will ensure that there are sufficient numbers of young trees to guarantee the survival of these woodlands.

Heading further north still in our look at upland woodlands, we arrive at the very

But it is not just the birds that are so special. There are 44 British beetle species that are mainly restricted to Scottish pinewoods, many of which rely on dead wood for their existence. A number of plants that were once common are now very local in their distribution, due to the reduction in pinewood area. Of five orchids regularly found, coralroot, creeping lady's tresses and lesser twayblade are noteworthy. Four species of wintergreen occur, including one-flowered wintergreen. This is the rarest of all the pinewood flowers and is only found in the Speyside woods.

The native pinewoods of Scotland are internationally recognised as being of prime conservation importance. They are generally believed to be closer to the original natural conditions than any other woodland habitat in Britain. For many years, the RSPB has been acquiring native pinewoods as a priority habitat. Since 1975, the RSPB has purchased eight pieces of land on Speyside totalling 12,800 ha (31,550 acres), based around the famous osprey site at Loch Garten. This area is now referred to as the Abernethy Forest Nature Reserve and incorporates 2,600 ha (6,400 acres) of native woodland, including 16% of the remaining 16,000 ha of native pine in Britain. As a result, the RSPB now owns most of the largest remaining tract of native Caledonian pinewood.

Buying land is only an initial step in protecting our native pinewoods. Further action has to take place to ensure that the woods will regenerate naturally. At Abernethy, seasonal grazing by sheep on the adjacent open moorland ceased in 1990. Detailed counts of deer populations revealed high numbers of both red and roe deer. Cull levels were established and over the next three years the red deer population was reduced by about 40% in the main woodland block. Subsequent monitoring revealed a 20% increase in the total number of established young trees. These results are very encouraging because they show that, even in a short period, appropriate management has been successful. In the long-term, the pinewood should increase to its former extent within the nature reserve boundaries.

At Inversnaid, another exciting native pinewood project is also underway. This nature reserve is situated at the southern extremity of the former Great Wood of Caledon, but the last Scots pine disappeared from the area a long time ago. In 1994, 24 ha (59 acres) of poor quality moorland were fenced off and, the following year, planting of Scots pine commenced. The seed is collected annually from nearby Glen Falloch, now the most southerly remnant of the Caledonian pine forest. This ensures that only local provenance is used, as well as conserving the Glen Falloch strain of Scots pine. Now that the area is protected from grazing, other tree species are naturally regenerating. The end result will be a pine dominated forest with a mosaic of birch, rowan, willow, hawthorn and perhaps aspen and holly.

It is not just the RSPB which is carrying out important conservation work with our native pinewoods. In 1992, the Forestry Commission published its own document for the future of pinewoods owned by Forest Enterprise. In an ambitious initiative, the Commission plans to create new Caledonian forest reserves covering more than 12,000 ha of countryside. Together with improvements to the Woodland Grant Scheme, the future of native pinewoods in Scotland is looking better than at any time during the last few hundred years.

Finally in our journey northwards, we come to the Highland birchwoods. They have suffered a history of exploitation, similar to other types of upland woodlands, but they show a number of special features. Birch is a relatively short-lived tree which produces vast amounts of seed every year. It can rapidly colonise ungrazed moorland, but it rarely regenerates within birchwoods. Thus you can find birchwoods developing in one area but degenerating in another close by.

From a bird point of view, upland birchwoods are generally regarded as being rather species poor. However, they make up for this by supporting probably the highest density of any breeding bird in Britain. The willow warbler is our commonest and most widespread summer

Golden eagle

visitor and birch woodland is its stronghold. It forms about one-third of the bird community there, outnumbering its nearest rival, the chaffinch, by three to one. Densities are highest in the north of Scotland and one woodland in Wester Ross supported an amazing 425 pairs per square kilometre. It is also interesting to note that birchwoods in this part of Scotland represent the closest approximation to the taiga of the Arctic.

Likewise, the flowering plants of this habitat include few rarities, although in the absence of grazing a good variety will develop. However, the wetter and more western sites are especially rich in oceanic bryophytes and lichens, and some will have luxuriant growths of ferns. There is also a very large number of insect species which are dependent on birch, and this is one reason for the high numbers of willow warblers.

There are in fact two types of birch that commonly grow in Britain – the silver birch and the downy birch, the latter being a more northerly species. A combination of attractive silvery bark, delicate fine-toothed leaves and a glorious autumn colour, makes the birch one of our prettiest trees.

Together with the golden brown colours of bracken and purple moor grass, birchwoods make many Highland glens in October a rich blend of autumnal colours.

Despite its name, the RSPB nature reserve at Insh Marshes contains some fine examples of birch woodland. They are located around the fringes of the marshes and include excellent stands of juniper understorey. And in the extreme north, the RSPB owns the most northerly remnant of natural woodland anywhere in Britain. This is Berriedale on the Orkney island of Hoy. Here, three hectares (seven acres) of birch, aspen and rowan woodland eke out an existence in the comparatively sheltered environment of a narrow river course. By excluding sheep grazing and with the help of some careful planting, this unique piece of woodland is slowly spreading.

Having started our journey in the south and finished it in our most northerly woodland, we have completed our look at Britain's main types of upland woodland. These surviving native woodlands are a priceless part of our national heritage, rich in wildlife and of great landscape and amenity value. Not only are they areas of outstandingly beautiful countryside, but they are an important and irreplaceable natural resource. These woods have evolved over many hundreds of years, during which time their immensely varied plant and animal communities have developed. Once lost, these woodlands cannot be replaced and today there is a growing realisation that these remnants are important to all of us and need to be conserved. The RSPB is one of the leading organisations in the conservation and management of our native upland woodlands and will continue to protect this unique and wonderful habitat.

Mike Trubridge

Pipistrelle bats thrive on Scotland's least popular insects – midges!

N Benvie (RSPB Images)

Up in the wilds

Freedom, peace, solitude and a brief escape to wilderness attract millions of people to drive and walk through moorlands each year. To the foreign visitor, our moorlands are an unfamiliar, characteristically British landscape. For the birdwatcher, they offer an exciting array of species typical of more northerly tundra areas, with many of these birds breeding at the most southerly edge of their world range.

At a distance, the bleak windswept land above the highest stone walls and fences, which enclose the sheep pasture and woodland of lower ground, might appear to be a true wilderness hardly touched by human hand. Perhaps disappointingly to the newcomer, nothing could be further from the truth.

The distribution of moorland in Britain, from Cornwall to Shetland, owes much to factors of geology, topography and climate. Without human intervention, however, our moorland landscape would largely be cloaked in a mantle of woodland. Only the coldest and highest peaks, the steepest cliffs and most windswept areas of the north would appear treeless, as they do today.

Moorland is, in fact, one of the oldest agricultural habitats in the country. The open nature of today's moorland was established to a large extent by the end of the Bronze Age. The rotting stumps of the original wild wood that once covered much of today's moorland area can still often be seen in places where streams cut through deep peat soils. Standing stones and stone circles scattered throughout upland areas give further evidence of the ancient settlement of the wild wood.

The expansion of animal husbandry and cultivation of crops gradually allowed

A Rouse (NHPA)

The RSPB fought to save Lurcher's Gully from ski development

certain plants of the woodland understorey to spread out into great clearings, and colonise abandoned cultivations. It is these, essentially woodland plants – heather, bilberry and crowberry – which remain today to give moorland its characteristic hues of purple and green.

During this period of early clearance, many moorland areas became quite densely settled and there are signs of cultivation of crops during the Iron Age, much higher up than would ever be attempted today. Thin, nutrient-poor upland soils could never sustain cultivation for long and soon became barren. At the same time, the lowland areas were steadily being cleared of forest and, as people began to leave the uplands, the cold, wet weather associated with these areas, coupled with poor

Author

Sean Reed *has worked as a Conservation Officer at the RSPB's North West Regional Office since 1991. He studied ecology at Leeds University, and has worked on wildlife reserves in Central and South America and as a management plan co-ordinator for the National Trust.*

drainage, led to the formation of the thick peat soils which underlie most of moorland Britain today. In the very north and west of Scotland, extremely high rainfalls and poor drainage over thousands of years have led to the development of expanses of wet, pool-studded peatlands, characterised by water-loving plants such as sphagnum moss and cotton grass and by a particularly spongy, squelchy feeling underfoot. Habitat of this kind, known as blanket bog, is limited worldwide to a few localities on oceanic coastlines such as the Caithness Flows of north-west Scotland and northern Scandinavia. If moorland can be described as a wilderness area, then this is it.

Golden plover in full breeding plumage

Opposite page: packhorse bridge over a Welsh moorland stream

M Lane (Woodfall Wild Images)

The RSPB's Forsinard Nature Reserve in Sutherland is one of the finest examples of this wet wilderness, and a trip in spring promises breeding bird specialities such as greenshanks, dunlins, golden plovers, merlins and hen harriers. Many birds can be seen from the road which runs through the nature reserve and good views of the bogs can be had from the train which stops right outside the visitor centre. A self-guided flagstone path leads the way past hundreds of bog pools teeming with sundews, bog bean and rare northern

dragonflies. The 7,670 ha (19,000 acre) nature reserve was mainly purchased in 1995 following an enormously successful public appeal. Management of the site now is mainly aimed at protecting the important areas of bog by damming old hill drains to raise water tables and minimising the draining effects of adjacent forestry. Good examples of blanket bog in Scotland can also be seen at the RSPB nature reserves of Lumbister and Fetlar in the Shetland Islands and Balranald in the Outer Hebrides.

The Scottish Flow Country is the main centre of breeding activity for one of Britain's rarest and most elegant birds, the greenshank. Greenshank nests are notoriously difficult to find as these birds are highly secretive at nesting time. It is easier to see them before and after nesting, feeding around blanket bog pools where insects abound. Unfortunately, the threats to the Scottish flows from drainage and forestry look set to remain. The RSPB will continue to gain recognition and protection for these most important breeding areas.

Blanket bog is not restricted to the far north and west of Scotland. The torrential rain which encourages the development of wet, boggy pools with actively growing sphagnum mosses – the basis of peat – can be found on high moorland areas throughout the country, forming the core of most large moorland blocks. These bogs offer rich rewards to those who are willing to trek to the moor tops on a fine day in spring. On reaching an area of blanket bog, often the first sign of bird life is the plaintive wail of a golden plover. It can take several minutes of scanning the tops of cotton grass hummocks and sphagnum mounds before the golden spangled bird is finally picked out. A lucky observer may even chance upon the male's complex looping song flight.

The dunlin's real stronghold is the north and west of Scotland, but it can be found in

most blanket bog areas of the central Pennines. The trilling display of a male dunlin in early spring sounds more like a mini-spaceship coming in to land than a bird and will certainly make anyone's birdwatching day. However, the most usual view of this dapper little bird is when a bird is flushed off the nest as you squelch your way through a high bog.

Apart from the northern and western isles and north-west coast of Scotland, where blanket bog can occur at sea level, blanket bogs are usually surrounded by what most people recognise as true upland 'moorland'. These grassy or heather-clad slopes are usually grazed by sheep. They are frequently managed for a single species, known throughout the world for its association with the commencement of the annual shooting season on 'the glorious twelfth' of August each year. British red grouse, an endemic sub-species of the continental willow grouse, have probably been hunted since Neolithic times, when they would have occurred at the treeline in the more mountainous and wet northerly areas of the country. While grouse populations are likely to have increased as their staple food source, heather, expanded into the cleared landscape of Bronze Age times, the real change in their fortunes came later. In the 19th century, the enclosure of land, the establishment of rail links with Scotland and the invention of the breech loading gun all helped make grouse shooting very popular. Many upland estates were given over to the production of heather for grouse.

Prior to this, moorland probably consisted of a mix of grass, scrub and heather, with individual moorland areas varying greatly depending on the different uses to which it was put. Many areas of England and Wales were once royal or private hunting forests, with red deer being the main quarry. These hunting 'forests' can still be recognised in the names of moorland areas such as the

C H Gomersall (RSPB Images)

Forest of Bowland and Forest of Rossendale in Lancashire, the Forests of Ettrick and Ross in Scotland and Radnor Forest in Wales. In the 13th century, the biggest source of red deer for the English kings' table was the Forest of Inglewood in Cumbria. Other moorland areas were grazed, either as commons such as Dartmoor and Exmoor or, in the Pennines, by flocks of sheep belonging to Cistercian monks. With the profits from the sale of wool, the monks built great abbeys in the moorlands of Yorkshire.

With the agricultural revolution, and improvements in stock breeding, there was a switch from grazing predominantly by cattle to sheep grazing. The change from cattle to sheep is notoriously associated with the Highland clearances between 1782 and 1854, when thousands of Scottish tenant crofters were evicted by their landlords. After the clearances, red deer were again hunted in many parts of the Scottish Highlands. A rapidly growing economy based on a thriving world empire, and the Enclosure Act which brought large areas of moorland into private control, created the conditions for the new fashion of grouse shooting to spread.

As it was not possible to breed grouse in captivity for release into the wild, the only

The heather-clad uplands are home to the red grouse

Opposite page: red deer stag on the Isle of Jura

way to ensure large enough grouse numbers for driven shoots across concealed 'butts' was to turn the moorland areas over to intensive heather production. This was achieved through the work of a rapidly growing number of gamekeepers, who began a system of rotational patchwork burning of heather to encourage the growth of the young heather shoots, which are the favoured food of red grouse. The young heather was interspersed with enough old heather to provide cover. Sheep numbers were controlled so that the young heather was not eaten away to be replaced by coarse grasses which cannot be eaten by grouse. Careful heather management, together with intensive predator control, meant that, by the late 1800s, grouse bags of over 1,000 brace per day were being achieved in the moors of the Peak District, Forest of Bowland and Yorkshire Dales. Unfortunately, in these early days, predator control included the destruction of all birds of prey. While the grouse population burgeoned under the stringent management regime, one of the most evocative of moorland birds, the hen harrier, was driven to extinction from the mainland of Britain, exiled in the northern and western isles of Scotland.

The heather-managed areas of moorland in upland Britain are among the richest for nesting birds. The newly burned areas provide nest sites for curlews and golden plovers, while the longer heather provides shelter for nesting meadow pipits, merlins and twites.

Two birds of prey common in moorland areas, the peregrine and the merlin, suffered a population crash in the 1960s. In both cases, the cause of the decline was the persistent organochlorine pesticides which had found their way into the food chain via smaller birds feeding, for example, on treated grain. This is an excellent example of how wildlife can help humans by acting as a 'canary down the coalmine', indicating the health of our environment. In this case, the problem identified with the peregrine population in particular, helped to secure the withdrawal of the most dangerous chemicals from agricultural use. Recent RSPB and British Trust for Ornithology (BTO) surveys have shown that both merlin and peregrine populations are thriving once again.

N Benvie

Crowberry

Opposite page: the UK's smallest falcon, the merlin, is a bird of the uplands

Breeding waders and twites can be found in particularly high densities on the lower slopes of heather moorland. Here, there is easy access to rich feeding grounds on the wet, rushy pastures and on the herb-rich hay meadows of the enclosed fields fringing the open moorland – often known as 'in-bye' land. Snipe, redshanks and curlews probe for food with their long bills in the wettest fields, nesting in the rushy clumps which are usually found there. Lapwings prefer more closely-grazed fields where they can use their large eyes to hunt for insects. Small colonies of breeding twites, nesting in adjacent moorland, home in on weedy, unimproved hay meadows which conceal an abundance of protein-rich seeds with which they feed their young. After breeding, once the hay meadows are cut, flocks of twites move to cattle-grazed pasture, roadsides and disturbed ground where they feed on the seeds of thistles and many other different kinds of weeds. They then move off to winter on coastal saltmarshes.

Peregrine falcon

A walk along the moorland-in-bye boundary, with its combination of moorland, agricultural and woodland habitats, can be particularly rewarding for the birdwatcher. Grey wagtails and dippers are easily seen along moorland streams, and whinchats occur in areas of bracken and scrub. Wheatears thrive in tightly-grazed sheep pasture, while ring ouzels feed in the wetter grasslands. Steep-sided, wooded moorland valleys can support a range of birds such as redstarts, wood warblers and pied flycatchers together with more familiar lowland birds such as blue tits and song thrushes.

M Hamblin (RSPB Images)

Displaying black grouse are a rarer sight on moorland

The intimate mosaic of moorland, woodland and agricultural habitats is also favoured by the black grouse, famed for the dramatic jousting display of males each spring at established grounds known as leks. Once occupying all moorland areas in the country, the range of this bird has been steadily contracting northwards throughout this century, so that its southernmost boundary is now found in the Yorkshire Dales. Unlike red grouse which can survive almost exclusively on heather, black grouse need the full range of habitats to provide essential food and shelter at different times of the year. The loss of just one of these components can lead to the demise of black grouse in an area.

The First World War heralded the end of the hey-day of moorland management for the red grouse. During the War, most moors went unmanaged and the economic depression of the following years meant that less capital was available for heather management. At this time, many moorland areas went out of grouse shooting and into sheep grazing. Within a few years, the heather of the moors to the north of Manchester and in many other areas had been replaced by grass-dominated sheep walk – the landscape which greets the visitor to this day.

Things were not improved, following the Second World War, by the desire to make Britain self-sufficient in food production, or by the introduction of production-led subsidies. The production-led system was intensified under the Common Agricultural Policy, which remains a major obstacle but also an opportunity to improve upland habitats for wildlife.

The continuing decline of the black grouse illustrates very well the major threats which all upland bird populations are facing. The moorlands and associated upland valleys for which Britain is so renowned have suffered, and continue to suffer, a rapid reduction in the range and abundance of wildlife during the 20th century.

Upland farms have become sheep production units, increasing their stocking capacity through drainage, re-seeding and artificially fertilising pastures. This has led to the replacement of areas of heather moor by grassy sheep walk and to a loss of the wet, rushy pastures, herb-rich hay meadows and areas of cultivated land on the moorland fringe, which are so important for birds. Technological advances, including the use of concentrated foods and machinery to take food up onto the hills, has enabled grazing of sheep on moorland throughout the winter in some areas. Heather is at its most vulnerable during the winter period and is easily destroyed by excessive grazing at this time, as shown by areas of heather destruction around winter feeding stations.

In the Peak District, it has been estimated that around a third of the heather coverage of the Park was lost between 1913 and 1981. In many parts of the South Pennines near Halifax and the moors north of Manchester, old grouse butts can be seen in grassland now heavily grazed by sheep, firm evidence of former heather moorland. This pattern is unfortunately repeated through much of upland England, Wales and Scotland.

In south-west England and Wales, grouse and other heather moorland species are now very scarce indeed, the bare green hills offering very little food or shelter for these specialist upland birds. Once reduced to low numbers by habitat destruction, the few remaining pockets of birds are much more vulnerable to predation by crows and foxes. The situation in Wales has been thoroughly documented in an RSPB report called *Silent Fields*. Another RSPB bird survey in the North Staffordshire moors suggests that the disappearance of breeding waders, witnessed in Wales, may be repeating itself here. This is reflected in a decline in the population of red grouse in many parts of the country and the northward contraction of the black grouse population.

The same factors which had conspired to damage populations of many characteristic moorland birds have allowed recoveries of

N Benvie

other populations. Notable here are increases in red kite and raven populations, helped by an increase in sheep carrion, an increased recognition of the need to protect birds of prey in general and a decline in the number of gamekeepers. Very recent expansions in the range of ravens and buzzards in the Pennines may further reflect an increased recognition of the importance of birds of prey and of their legal protection, probably as a result of RSPB publicity and the Government campaign against the illegal poisoning of wildlife.

In general terms, it is safe to say that the fortunes of birds of prey on moorland areas have slowly improved during the 20th century, with one notable exception – the hen harrier. This bird began to recolonise mainland Scotland just before the Second World War, thanks to the new forestry plantations which provided suitable habitat on unkeepered land. Their lot improved still further during the War, as gamekeepers were called up into the Armed Forces. It was not until the late 1960s and early 1970s that the hen harrier managed to regain a foothold in England. The total population of hen harriers in

Common sundew, an insect-eating plant of moorland bogs

Wheatear

L Campbell (NHPA)

Red deer stag

birds which have typified them for so long and inspired so many? Are they to be replaced by miles of coarse grass grazed by millions of sheep? Well, the picture is not quite so bleak. Through the research and lobbying work of the RSPB and other conservation organisations, the value of Britain's moorland for wildlife is now well recognised. It is no accident that nine out of 10 National Parks designated to date are in upland areas.

The Government's nature conservation advisers have designated large areas of upland moorland as Sites of Special Scientific Interest (SSSIs) and have given these areas international recognition through the designation of Special Protection Areas (SPAs) and Special Areas of Conservation (SACs). RSPB bird survey work has been invaluable to many of these designations, and the RSPB will continue to encourage and support moves for further designations. More recently, the Ministry of Agriculture, Fisheries and Food (MAFF) has introduced the new agri-environment schemes such as the Moorland Scheme and the Environmentally Sensitive Area Schemes (ESAs), which pay farmers to maintain or reduce sheep stocking levels rather than to increase them. Much remains to be done, however, to turn production-led subsidies into those which benefit wildlife and rural communities: at the moment the battle for birds is still being lost.

Although heather moorland is of high wildlife value, the wide dispersal of the birds makes it very difficult to protect large proportions of the country's upland wildlife through reserve purchases.

Britain is now estimated to be in the region of 600 breeding pairs, but only around 16 of these are found in England. RSPB research has shown that due to persecution, hen harriers nest less successfully on keepered grouse moors than on other moorland and in adjacent young forestry plantations. Human persecution of this species on grouse moors is preventing it from occupying its natural range within the country. Eradicating persecution of the hen harrier and returning it to its natural range remains a high priority conservation action for the RSPB.

While production-led subsidies of farming have encouraged the deterioration of much of the uplands as a wildlife habitat, it has been greatly exacerbated by new conifer plantations and overgrazing by deer in Scotland. The more recently identified problems of acid rain and global warming could potentially pose even greater threats to our uplands. So, are Britain's hills destined to become stripped of the peat, heather and magical

The RSPB does, however, own and manage several nature reserves in Scotland, which support heather moorland, usually in association with wetland, blanket bog and woodland habitats. Although too many to mention here, examples include Killiecrankie in Tayside, Abernethy in the Highlands – famous for its Loch Garten osprey watch site, a number of large moorland nature reserves in Orkney, and Lumbister and Fetlar in the Shetland Islands. Heather moorland is also found on some nature reserves in Wales and England. Notable examples in Wales include Dinas and Lake Vyrnwy in Powys; and in England Haweswater and Geltsdale in Cumbria.

On all upland RSPB nature reserves, managers control stock numbers in order to protect heather and allow upland woodland areas to regenerate. Traditional low intensity farming practices are promoted to benefit moorland birds. The RSPB has a clear vision for the future of British moorland. It wants to see the maintenance and expansion of blanket bogs, heather moorland and the associated in-bye habitats which fringe them. History has shown us that the nature of British moorland has changed radically over the centuries, dictated by changes in the socio-economic conditions prevalent at the time. The RSPB's challenge will be to ensure that, as economic conditions change in the next millennium, the bird species for which Britain is so important have a secure future.

Farming is likely to dominate land-use in the uplands for the foreseeable future, and will be influenced increasingly by world trade conditions. If upland habitats are to be maintained and enhanced by extending heather cover and creating wildlife-rich in-bye land, upland agricultural support will need to be directed to this end even more, and less towards the support of

D Woodfall (Woodfall Wild Images)

Bilberry

intensive sheep production. While upland farming is now dependent upon economic support, conservation remains dependent upon upland farming. If a sustainable future is to be secured for the uplands, environmentally sensitive practices must be financially attractive to the upland farming communities, which manage the land. A thriving rural economy is vital to the successful conservation of upland birds.

Personal mobility is likely to continue to increase and greater leisure use of the uplands is predicted. Careful planning will be necessary to ensure that fragile habitats are not damaged further. Recreational use must be sustainable and integrated into the rural economy along with new industry and forestry. The RSPB will continue to work to ensure that upland birds always have a place in our lives.

Curlew

Surrounded by water

D Tomlinson (RSPB Images)

The Old Man of Hoy

There are thousands of islands around our coastline and each has its own unique quality. However, there are some islands off the north and west coasts of Scotland where farming practices such as crofting and a special habitat known as machair can continue to produce some of the most diverse and important areas for birds and botany in the UK. And it is here that some of the RSPB's own nature reserves enable the visitor to experience a little island magic of their own.

In a wider European context, machair is a very scarce habitat indeed and is restricted in its distribution to the Atlantic fringes of western Scotland and Ireland.

Ask many birdwatchers where they would choose to be on a sunny day in May or June and they would probably name a favourite island in the Hebrides, Orkney or maybe Shetland. These island groups and others around our shoreline hold a special magic which draws visitors back year after year. There is a strong sense of 'getting away from it all' for the visitor, but it is usually the work on the land by the island residents that make islands so important for birds and other wildlife.

This importance for nature conservation has been reflected over the years by the RSPB's own nature reserves acquisition policy. Now some of our most important and threatened birds are thriving on our island nature reserves; birds like corncrakes on the Isle of Coll and red-necked phalaropes on Fetlar.

Machair occurs on the Outer Hebrides, the Uists, Benbecula, Barra and Vatersay and in the Inner Hebrides on Tiree. It is a series of habitats which combine to form the rich conditions which breeding waders and other wildlife find so attractive. If you were to land on the beach at Balranald on North Uist and walk inland, you would first encounter a bank of sand dunes with occasional damp hollows or 'slacks' which hold their own special flora. Crofters may use these areas for grazing their cattle, while the dry machair beyond is the best area for crop cultivation and better grazing. The soil here is largely shellsand often fertilised by seaweed from the beaches over the generations. Beyond this lies the in-bye land. On some of these fields, hay is grown and yellow flag irises provide early cover in spring for corncrakes.

Author

David Sexton *studied in Virginia and received a degree in anthropology. He also monitored the local bald eagle population and worked on reintroducing peregrines. On his return to the UK, he worked for the RSPB on the sea eagle reintroduction project. He is now the head of the RSPB's reserves section in Scotland.*

Walking on further inland, we leave the rich machair of the coast. The soils become thinner still and the ground is dominated by blanket boglands.

This marvellous mosaic of habitats, so heavily influenced by the Atlantic, provides ideal conditions for a wealth of wildlife. There is nothing to compare with a visit to these areas in June. Birdsfoot trefoil, clovers, daisy, buttercup and bedstraws carpet the dry machair, while saxifrage, wild pansy and storksbill are more common on the cultivated machair. The bogs and pools provide suitable conditions for orchids, marsh marigolds and bogbean.

But it is also for the densities of breeding birds that many people visit. Each species has its own particular section of machair to nest on while feeding on others. Oystercatchers and ringed plovers may lay their eggs on the pebbly sections of the cultivated machair, but will feed along the shoreline. Lapwings, meanwhile, prefer the sheep and cattle grazed pastures for nesting and feeding while the screeching trill of displaying dunlins can be heard from the damp, boggy grasslands. They too may feed along the beach itself.

Your visit to one of these areas is bound to cause that 'sentinel of the marshes', the redshank, to warn others of your presence. Perched alertly on a fence post above the pools and ditches, it is one of the characteristic birds of these superb island habitats. Breeding populations of birds such as snipe are now largely confined to nature reserves in England and Wales; it is vital therefore, that the waders of north-west Europe continue to find well-managed, crofted machair on these Atlantic fringe islands.

Islands throughout the UK, or nature reserves on them can often be some of the most expensive land for the RSPB to buy,

simply because of the unquantifiable 'island factor'. Millionaires and bidders from overseas take a special interest in remote island hideaways. They can also be expensive reserves to manage. Transport of materials or goods to and from the islands can be time-consuming and costly, and has to be taken into consideration when deciding whether to establish an island nature reserve. It is only after hard-headed valuations and site assessments are completed that we can allow ourselves the indulgence of actually enjoying the special qualities of our island nature reserves.

J Narkhan (RSPB Images)

Wild pansies flourish in machair habitat and on some islands

With so many RSPB island nature reserves to choose from, we will look at just a few in detail, how they are managed, and maybe we can whet your appetite for a visit or even a spell as a voluntary warden.

Loch Gruinart Nature Reserve on Islay in the Inner Hebrides is one of the RSPB's most important in terms of habitats and species and perhaps also the most complex. It was acquired in the mid-1980s when the winter goose damage to farmland crops and the 'birds versus jobs' debate was at its height. Islay is the most important wintering site in the world for barnacle geese and white-fronted geese which nest in Greenland.

Gannet

The RSPB acquired 1,667 ha (4,000 acres) of land with the intention of providing a safe refuge for these internationally important birds which, at that time, were still being culled under licence. The plan was to farm the land 'in house' by providing grass for the geese. This would keep them at the reserve for longer and so relieve some of the pressure caused by geese grazing on grass which other farmers needed for their own livestock.

A Williams (NHPA)

Scottish island reserves are vital to the future of the corncrake

The combination of this action by the RSPB, and management schemes introduced by the Government adviser on nature conservation, Scottish Natural Heritage (SNH), has meant that much of the controversy over geese has now subsided. Indeed, the wildlife spectacle they produce between October and April is now viewed rather differently – and even as a benefit to the island economy in terms of 'green' tourism. While 20–30,000 geese will always be a part of island life and some conflict will resurface from time to time, they are also a resource which can be enjoyed by visitors who will stay in Islay's many hotels, guest houses and bed and breakfasts. The dawn and dusk flights of the geese to and from their roosting sites on Loch Gruinart and Loch Indaal are a breathtaking sight and more than enough to ease the chill of a winter's day on Islay.

However, as the need to 'farm for geese' began to lessen by the end of the 1980s, a new conservation priority was rapidly approaching over the horizon.

Corncrakes were formerly a widespread and common species throughout the UK. By the late 1980s, their range had drastically reduced and they were largely extinct from the UK, with fewer than 500 calling males recorded in 1993. The corncrake survived in the north and west islands of the UK, mostly on the Outer Hebrides and on Tiree. Their decline was caused by mechanised and more intensive farming practices, including the loss of hay meadows, which has reduced the amount of tall vegetation available in the summer for nesting, feeding and cover. Mechanised grass cutting now means fields are cut earlier, faster and within a shorter period. It has led to more nests and young being destroyed – a problem exacerbated by the modern technique of mowing fields from the outside towards the centre. Corncrakes seemed in terminal decline. They became listed as a globally threatened species. Could Loch Gruinart respond and adapt its management now to help save the species?

At about the same time, in 1991, the RSPB purchased part of the Coll Estate on the Isle of Coll to create a 'corncrake recovery area'. Corncrakes on Coll had also been declining, but the reductions had been slower and the potential existed to reverse the decline. However, whereas on Islay we had our own livestock and machinery, we did not have that degree of control on Coll.

Our approach on Coll was to try, where possible, to divide the nature reserve up between four or five neighbouring farmers who expressed an interest in increasing their grazing. So, by setting up annual grazing and hay or silage cropping lets, the essential habitat management for corncrakes was underway. We were able to tailor the lets to suit the corncrakes' needs without seriously inconveniencing our graziers, or if it did, their rent would be adjusted accordingly. For example, most livestock needed to be off the key corncrake meadows by March or April to give time for the grass to grow tall enough to conceal the secretive corncrakes. Small areas known as 'corncrake corners' or strips of fields along a wall or ditch would be fenced off and grazing animals excluded from the turn of the year. This allowed time for the essential early cover of nettles, cow parsley and sweet cicely to grow up ready for the corncrakes' arrival in late April.

Neighbouring farmers followed the progress of the corncrake experiment with great interest. It was a bird many Collachs (islanders of Coll) knew from days of old. A bird they remembered fondly, despite the occasional sleepless night caused by the strange rasping call of the corncrake which proclaims its presence mostly between 1 and 3 am!

At harvest time, farmers agreed not to begin cutting their fields before 1 August, by which time most corncrake chicks are at least mobile. Even more importantly, they changed their cutting pattern, so that instead of cutting from the outside inwards, leaving corncrake families trapped in the middle of the field, farmers cut from the inside out, or in strips across the field; both techniques allow corncrakes to escape in safety to the edges of the field.

Elsewhere on the islands, a Corncrake Initiative Scheme was launched by the RSPB and SNH and supported by the Scottish Crofters' Union. Away from our nature reserves, this gave the remaining corncrakes a chance to survive. Farmers and crofters were paid an incentive to manage their fields in a corncrake friendly manner. It was beginning to work.

By 1995, the nature reserve on Coll had witnessed a five-fold increase in calling corncrakes. They had increased from six

C H Gomersall (RSPB Images)

Puffin

when the reserve was purchased in 1991 to 31 in the 1995 season. Even more importantly, the overall island population was beginning to recover, especially in areas where management agreements were in place. Coll was rapidly becoming known as the 'Corncrake Island' with a BBC TV programme made about the island and nature reserve and the Prince of Wales making a summer visit to see the corncrake management for himself. Corncrakes appeared on Coll mugs and T-shirts on sale in island stores and visitors stayed on the island in bed and breakfasts in the hope of hearing or even seeing this elusive bird.

Meanwhile, down the coast on Islay, Loch Gruinart's operation had changed gear and

Guillemot

C H Gomersall (RSPB Images)

ferally by wintering on the Coll reserve and then 'migrating' back to Mull each spring. Occasionally a lone wild snow goose may turn up on the islands causing the wardens to cry that this one is 'genuine'. But is it . . ?

There are so many nature reserves to choose from within the island complex which makes up Orkney that it's impossible to choose a favourite. It is perhaps the spectacular seabird colonies which appeal to most. Marwick Head Nature Reserve on Mainland Orkney offers easily viewable seabirds with densely packed breeding guillemots and razorbills with shags and fulmars also present in good numbers. Other islands with impressive seacliffs and seabirds are Hoy (with an RSPB nature reserve at the north end) and Copinsay. North Hoy has the added drama of a possible encounter with a great skua defending its chicks and a view across to the famous sea stack, the Old Man of Hoy. Here, a few puffins breed on the uppermost reaches, emerging cautiously from their burrows on the alert for peregrines or skuas patrolling these cliffs – some of the highest in the UK.

its management plan was adjusted to take account of the reserve's potential for corncrakes. From none in 1990, the nature reserve recorded nine calling males in 1995, either on the reserve or on its immediate boundaries. Loch Gruinart too had maximised its provision of early cover for corncrakes and adjusted its cutting and harvesting.

This close look at Coll and Islay shows how our island nature reserves can make a real contribution towards saving our most important and threatened birds and adjust to ever changing priorities. By the way, if you see a flock of 40 or so beautiful snow geese on Coll one winter, do enjoy them but don't get too excited that you have discovered an unprecedented arrival from the Arctic. These birds were once reared on the neighbouring Isle of Mull and now live

Other islands on Orkney with RSPB nature reserves offer gentler but no less impressive birdwatching. Rousay offers the chance to watch red-throated divers and maybe hen harriers, while neighbouring Egilsay has some impressive wader and wildfowl populations on the botanically-rich marshes. Egilsay is also likely to become the corncrake capital of Orkney, where careful RSPB management, in association with island farmers will eventually enable Egilsay to 'export' its corncrakes to new suitable locations on other Orkney islands. It is only thanks to the less intensive and environmentally friendly farming techniques employed on Egilsay to date that corncrakes have clung on in these northern isles at all.

For some people, their favourite island in Orkney is Papa Westray or 'Papay' where the RSPB has a nature reserve over the North Hill Site of Special Scientific Interest (SSSI) by agreement with the local grazing committee. A summer walk across the maritime heath in search of *Primula scotica* – the tiny pink Scottish primrose – accompanied by a disapproving chorus of arctic terns and the occasional smack on the head by an angry arctic skua makes for a memorable day out. A visit to 'Papay' is not complete without time spent at Fowlcraig – a superb little inlet with clear blue water and a seabird colony where kittiwakes nest at eye level and guillemots fly underwater in search of sandeels. Ponder too that this was the last known site in the UK where great auks survived.

Back on Mainland Orkney, the Birsay Moors Nature Reserve is a prime example of heather moorland with all its associated wildlife. Much moorland in Orkney has been agriculturally 'improved' by reseeding former heather with grassland for grazing, so the nature reserves such as Birsay are all the more important. Good populations of curlews, short-eared owls and hen harriers survive as do red grouse and golden plovers. The Loons Nature Reserve has a hide overlooking a wetland area where pintails and other ducks may be seen and breeding waders abound. The to-ing and fro-ing from coast to marsh of kittiwakes, in their annual search for muddy nest material, is worth watching here.

North beyond Orkney, in the land of the 'simmer dim' lie the islands of Shetland. Lying closer to the Arctic Circle than to London, the Norse influence in Shetland culture is everywhere, from island names to local bird names, to street names in the capital, Lerwick. The RSPB has several nature reserves in Shetland, the most famous of which is probably Fetlar, forever engraved in ornithological history as the first place in the British Isles where snowy owls nested in 1967. These formidable arctic predators nested annually feeding on rabbits, whimbrels and other wader chicks, and were guarded round the clock by the RSPB and the islanders. They soon became one of Shetland's major tourist attractions. With the crash in the rabbit population due to myxomatosis, the snowy owls ceased breeding in 1975, although the descendants of that pioneering pair could still be seen well into the 1990s. Snowy owls continue to appear in Shetland most years, so maybe one day history will repeat itself.

M Lane (Woodfall Wild Images)

Red-necked phalaropes are a speciality of the island of Fetlar

Meanwhile, the whimbrels are not sorry at their passing and their beautiful distinctive call is a common sound from the tundra-like, boulder-strewn serpentine heaths of Fetlar. The bird that people still travel to Fetlar to see is the exquisite red-necked phalarope, another species more common in the Arctic. Phalaropes have made use of old peat diggings by crofters which, when the digging of peat is over, often fill with water and sphagnum and provide ideal nesting habitat.

The hide overlooking the Mires of Funzie (pronounced Finnie) is an ideal spot to sit and watch for phalaropes. Perhaps the

Short-eared owl

N Bervie (RSPB Images)

Kittiwake

The wreck of the tanker MV *Braer*, which sank off Quendale Bay in 1993, is not far away and serves as a salutary reminder of the fragile state of these internationally important waters and coasts.

Elsewhere in Scotland, the RSPB has a number of island reserves scattered around the coast. Fidra in the Firth of Forth was bought from the Northern Lighthouse Board amidst much speculation over its connections with Robert Louis Stevenson and *Treasure Island*. The media had a field day, but the link remains tenuous. Fidra has an expanding puffin population as well as the other auks, shags, gulls, kittiwakes, eiders and fulmars. Boat trips visit from nearby North Berwick where trips out to the privately-owned Bass Rock and its gannet colony can also be arranged.

posse of brightly coloured females chasing the harassed males in courtship, or the male alarm-calling around the tiny chicks if a predator is nearby, will attract your attention to them. The phalaropes feed along the rocky shores of the Loch of Funzie. After a major hatch of flies, you can sit on a boulder at the water's edge and have phalaropes feeding at your feet. It is quite simply an unforgettable experience.

Fetlar has its seabirds too, but other sites such as the National Nature Reserve of Hermaness on the neighbouring island of Unst are more spectacular. Hermaness has its gannets (and an occasional black-browed albatross called Albert which strayed here one year from the Southern Atlantic and now thinks it's a gannet), while Sumburgh Head on the southern tip of Shetland Mainland has some very viewable puffins. The RSPB has established a seabird viewing site at Sumburgh where guillemots, fulmars, razorbills, kittiwakes, shags and puffins jostle for space. Out at sea, minke or killer whales or dolphins are an bonus for the patient watcher.

Other islands in the Firth of Forth are important tern nesting areas, but most are inaccessible. Coquet Island off the Northumbrian coast and Horse Island off Ayrshire have had nesting terns, gulls and eiders, but gulls eased out terns from the latter in the 1980s.

The RSPB nature reserve at South Stack on Anglesey in North Wales is dramatic and exciting. The lucky visitor will see choughs, peregrines, ravens and a thriving seabird colony.

Further south off the Pembrokeshire coast lies Ramsey Island, another important refuge for choughs and seabirds. Ramsey is looked after all year by a mainland warden, but staff are present on the island itself in summer to welcome visitors and to carry out essential habitat management tasks. Sheep, red deer and rabbits help maintain the grassland for probing chough beaks, while the dramatic steep rocky headlands and secluded beaches allow grey seals to pup in the autumn in safety. Ramsey offers that

Red-throated diver

island magic quality – that feeling of escape and tranquillity away from busy tourist routes on the mainland. A pod of porpoises in the Sound seen from the boat on the trip over is definitely the icing on the cake.

Havergate Island Nature Reserve off the Suffolk coast is famous as the site where avocets first returned to breed in England. Now avocets are well established and breeding on many mainland reserves including Minsmere, Titchwell and Elmley.

Islands are often associated with either the re-establishment or sadly the last refuges for some of our rarest and most threatened birds: the avocets at Havergate, the snowy owls on Fetlar, roseate terns in the Forth islands and even the white-tailed sea eagles on the Isle of Rum National Nature Reserve owned by Scottish Natural Heritage, and, of course, one of the RSPB's highest conservation priorities – the corncrakes on Islay, Coll, Tiree, the Uists and Orkney.

These islands around our coast and the nature reserves some of them contain are important for so much of our bird life and wildlife, often because they may be remote and difficult of access. We must be careful not to undermine the sanctuary which this remoteness provides. Island tourist bodies market their islands as secluded, peaceful, 'away from it all' havens and few of us can resist their allure. Some areas, like the Ardnamurchan peninsula in the Highlands, are marketed as 'almost an island' and also promise remoteness, wildness and a wealth of wildlife.

Our island nature reserves protect an impressive array of species and habitats, many of them severely threatened elsewhere in the UK. Let us hope that in our wish to escape from it all, we do not damage that unique island magic which will draw us back time and time again.

David B. Sexton

W S Paton (RSPB Images)

Tens of thousands of gannets nest on the island reserve of Grassholm

Making the most of reserves

Our nature reserves provide us with a unique opportunity to spread our conservation messages to a wide range of people – members and their families as well as decision-makers and land managers.

The main purpose of RSPB nature reserves is to safeguard and manage important habitats for birds and wildlife. However, a subsidiary but important aim has been to attract visitors to most of our reserves in order to enhance people's appreciation of wildlife and help them understand the need for conserving habitats. The scale of this attraction is indicated by the fact that in any one year RSPB nature reserves can receive a total of over one million visitors.

There are of course the favourites for people to visit and the RSPB has concentrated on providing good facilities to enhance the visitor experience at these popular sites. Some nature reserves by their sheer remoteness or vulnerability are not suitable for large numbers of people who may cause undue disturbance, say to nesting tern colonies on Coquet Island.

Opportunism has often dictated the siting and style of reserve visitor centres. The cliff-top folly at South Stack was converted to an excellent observatory of the auks nesting on ledges below, as well as the choughs and peregrines on this Anglesey headland. Loch Garten visitor centre grew when one of the first pairs of ospreys to recolonise the Scottish Highlands chose to nest there. The timber observatory is now equipped with mounted telescopes and a closed circuit TV focused on the nest. In 1989, an ideal opportunity arose to create another visitor centre with the purchase of Pulborough Brooks, West Sussex, which came with a traditional but dilapidated barn, now a fully equipped centre.

The facilities on our most popular nature reserves are there to improve the enjoyment of all our visitors but

C H Gomersall (RSPB Images)

arguably the most important of our visitors are young people. If we do not believe that the next generation will make better stewards of the environment, the RSPB's work has no value. From its earliest days, the RSPB has a proud record of bringing young people to its nature reserves to inspire them to become committed to the RSPB's aims.

Children have a natural affinity with and curiosity about natural history and the RSPB seeks to provide a means to fulfil this curiosity. The RSPB runs a sophisticated network of educational programmes on nature reserves throughout the UK, satisfying the enquiring mind of over 50,000 schoolchildren each year.

The RSPB believes that every child visiting one of these nature reserves is a potential environmental decision-maker of the future, and we are committed to making each reserve visit as memorable, enjoyable and educational as possible. In order to achieve this, our frontline troops are 75 teacher naturalists who teach visiting school groups on RSPB nature reserves.

Author

Andy Simpson *qualified as a teacher before working for the Wildfowl & Wetlands Trust centre at Martin Mere. In 1980, he became a regional education officer for the RSPB. Now Education Policy Manager, he influences Government policies in favour of the environment.*

To generate long-term interest and enthusiasm, it is necessary to allow children to discover things for themselves rather than being informed about them from another source.

First Nature is one of our most successful programmes. It is the first nationally available field teaching unit, designed specifically for children aged 5-7. *First Nature* is based on the idea of encouraging children to use their senses to discover the fascinating world of natural history. When children visit the nature reserve, they are given the *First Nature* bag which contains a series of coloured envelopes and articles they will need. The teacher naturalist then takes them on a sensory walk in which 'eyes', 'ears', 'noses' and touch are all used in a structured way. A good example of this process is the use of a 'listening jewel'. This is what happens:

'Did you hear that?'
'What?' ask John and Craig.
Chris, the guide, leads the children over to a gap in the hedge.
'Yes, I thought so. Over there – a wren.'
The children peer into the bushes as the tiny bird flits from branch to branch.

'I know what we need', says Chris, 'we need something that will help us to listen in to things, to hear the sounds all around us. Wouldn't it be brilliant if we could find all sorts of creatures just by stopping and using our ears?'

The group gathers round as Chris reaches into his bag and pulls out a beautiful round marble.

'This is a listening jewel. If you use it properly, it will help you hear all sorts of amazing things. What you have to do is put the jewel in your hand, grasp it tightly, then close your eyes and most important of all, keep quiet. If you do all of these things, the power of the jewel will work and you'll start to hear things. Shall we have a go?'

Chris passes a 'jewel' to everyone in the group.

'Looks like a marble to me', whispers Wendy.
'Yes, it does look like a marble, but it's actually a jewel given to us by a special friend so that we can help people like yourselves to use your ears.'

The group is organised. The children stand facing Chris, 'jewels' clenched tightly in their hands. 'Clasp the jewels tightly, close your eyes, keep quiet and listen . . .'
The group stands quiet. To their right, the wren sings, to their left in the distance a lorry trundles along a busy road, the breeze rustles the leaves of the hawthorn above their heads. Thirty seconds pass.

'OK, open your eyes', whispers Chris, 'What sort of things did you hear?'
'Birds', calls out Jatinder.
'Yes , that's right. Whereabouts?'
Three hands point to the bushes where the wren was singing.
'Anything else? What about the rumbling in the distance?'
The group carries on talking about the different sounds. Chris tells the group that sometimes, if they listen long enough, they will be able to hear the trees whispering to each other!
'. . . and remember', adds Chris to finish off, 'you don't need listening jewels like these to hear things. Some say the real secret, the real magic, is just to stop and be quiet.'

First Nature has been hugely successful and has received great praise from both the environmental movement and from teachers visiting the reserves.

Enviro-probe for secondary children gives them a chance to see and understand real wildlife habitats by scientific investigation. For example, they use scientific apparatus to investigate light levels, noise levels, moisture levels, ground density, oil pH levels in order to understand the nature of pressures upon the soil they are testing.

The RSPB undertakes extensive research to find out whether our reserve education programmes are meeting the needs of teachers, the interest of children and the conservation objectives of the RSPB. We are confident that, in all these areas, we are succeeding and our investment in the environmental decision-makers of the future is sound.

Farming on reserves

The majority of the RSPB's lowland wet grassland nature reserves depend on the continuation of traditional farming practices. Likewise, where we seek to re-create wet grasslands on land which has earlier been drained, ploughed and cultivated with arable crops, reintroducing traditional farming practices is vital to creating the right conditions for a wide range of breeding and wintering waterfowl.

Almost 10% of the RSPB's land, spread through 61 nature reserves, is subject to some form of grassland letting. Most are licences which are renewed on an annual basis, giving us flexibility to modify the dates between which grazing is allowed and the stocking density which is so critical in providing the right type of grass. Because many of the nature reserves are subject to winter flooding with some floodwater held on the site into the spring and early summer, grass growth does not start vigorously until quite late in the season. Thus, cattle are usually not let into fields known or expected to have breeding waders until perhaps mid-June; this minimises the risks of trampling nests or wader chicks.

In an average summer, there may be about 5,500 cattle on our nature reserves, most on the Ouse and Nene Washes in Cambridgeshire (2,000 and 450 respectively) and West Sedgemoor, Somerset (1,000).
In the western half of the UK, where there are high numbers of livestock, it is generally not difficult to find graziers with sufficient cattle to graze our reserves. However, in eastern Britain, where arable cultivation dominates, graziers may travel considerable distances, from Shropshire to Norfolk for example. As a result, wardens often provide a herding service over cattle whose owners are distant from the reserve, frequently becoming quite skilled in livestock husbandry in the process.

Cattle are not the only domesticated animals used for conservation management. We also have about 2,500 sheep on our lowland grassland sites, for example Elmley in Kent, Old Hall Marshes in Essex and Strumpshaw Fen in Norfolk. Sheep tend

C H Gomersall (RSPB Images)

Barnacle geese on Loch Gruinart

to produce a shorter, more even sward, much liked by wildfowl species, including wigeons, brent geese and bean geese.

Mechanical harvesting of grass to provide winter fodder to livestock is an important alternative to grazing. On some nature reserves, a few traditional hay meadows are cut very late in the season, in July or August after the flowering plants have gone to seed. West Sedgemoor and Strumpshaw Fen have some of the finest examples.

As a general rule, the RSPB prefers farmers to farm on our nature reserves, providing appropriate tenancy or licence arrangements can be used. Two significant exceptions are Loch Gruinart on Islay and Geltsdale on the Cumbria/Northumberland border.

At Loch Gruinart, the RSPB has run its own farming operation (cattle and sheep) since it bought the area. Not only have numbers of wintering barnacle and Greenland white-fronted geese on the nature reserve increased steadily (maximum numbers from 11,000 to 18,000 and from 600 to 1,300 respectively), but so too have numbers of breeding waders, with particularly high densities of lapwings and redshanks. Now that geese are more readily accepted by other farmers on their fields in winter (aided by goose management payments from Scottish Natural Heritage), we have been able to diversify our management to benefit other key species, especially corncrakes which have increased from none in 1990 to nine in 1995.

The other nature reserve where the RSPB owns significant numbers of livestock, albeit for the benefit of heather moorland, is Geltsdale. The RSPB has had a wardening and access agreement over 11,000 acres of heather moorland and rough grassland at Geltsdale for many years, but in 1991 we had the opportunity to purchase about 1,000 acres of that area, giving us the chance to carry out more active land management on the reserve. The purchase of moorland which has traditionally been grazed by sheep usually entails buying the resident flock of sheep, which are 'hefted' to the site, that is, they stay within the area of moor on which they are born and bred and do not require fencing to stop them wandering to other adjacent moors.

Thus, the RSPB came to purchase its first flock of 500 hill sheep. The first management decision was to reduce sheep numbers to reduce overgrazing of heather. Lambing the flock on the in-bye pasture, together also with a programme of bracken-spraying on the lower hill slopes has already made dramatic improvements to the condition of the heather on the site.

Financial considerations

Not only does farming on RSPB nature reserves help us to achieve our conservation objectives, but there are also financial benefits. Income from grazing licences and tenancies is increasing as we expand our landholdings.

Furthermore, we are often able to benefit from environmental or countryside grant-aid schemes, as frequently our own management objectives and prescriptions relate closely to those laid down by the Government.

Provided that conservation objectives are always given high priority, it is possible for nature reserve management to generate income from other by-products such as the sale of firewood or wood chippings from woodland thinning or coppicing, the sale of Christmas trees from coniferous woods or the sale of reed for thatching from reedbeds. Although these operations are generally on a small scale, they also provide some local employment as well as bringing income to the RSPB. Finally, it is worth mentioning that the management of a large estate of almost a million acres involves a very wide range of other income-producing opportunities from the letting of land or rights over land. Pipeline easements, fishing and boating licences, mooring rights, a military training range and observation post, crofts, farms and houses are but a few examples of other activities that subsist happily alongside the management of some of Britain's finest nature reserves under the stewardship of RSPB staff.

Geoffrey Osbon

Graham Hirons

Ynys-hir Nature Reserve

Our nature reserves

There are over 100 RSPB nature reserves all over the UK which can be visited by both members and non-members. The following pages will hopefully give you a taste of the variety of habitats the RSPB is conserving for wildlife.

We have highlighted the most popular nature reserves and given more detailed information on how to get there as well as what you can expect to see when you arrive.

The RSPB is committed to minimising the environmental impact of transport. Car sharing with friends cuts the cost of fuel and mileage, reduces parking pressure and, of course, pollution. If possible, use public transport when visiting reserves.

This is by no means a comprehensive list of information about our nature reserves. If you require specific details, it is worth contacting one of our regional or country offices (addresses given at the back of this book).

After reading the previous chapters, we hope you will be encouraged to visit our nature reserves and see some of our work at first-hand. Buying and managing nature reserves is a huge part of the RSPB's work and vital in the conservation of a wide variety of wildlife throughout the UK.

Please check the following pages for details of those nature reserves you can visit.

Key

♿ Disabled access

I Information leaflet about the nature reserve available

P Car parking

S Shop

🚼🚼 Toilets

ABERNETHY FOREST/ LOCH GARTEN, HIGHLAND

NH/978184 ♿ **I P S**

Visiting
The forest reserve, which includes the famous osprey site, is off the A95 between Aviemore and the villages of Boat of Garten and Nethybridge. Aviemore is the nearest railway station, 14 km (8.5 miles) from Loch Garten.

Location and habitat
Abernethy Forest Nature Reserve has a number of habitats including moorland, peatland, bog and loch and one of the largest remnants of the rare native Caledonian pine forest. The pinewoods, established some 8,000 years ago, have been felled and replanted in the last 200 years. Altogether the nature reserve is spread across more than 12,000 ha (30,000 acres).

Birds
Ospreys are now familiar at Loch Garten. Evening roosts on Loch Garten are a wonderful sight with goldeneyes, red-breasted mergansers and large numbers of gulls in spring, and goosanders and up to 2,000 greylag geese in the autumn. The Caledonian pine houses populations of species such as the crested tit, treecreeper, goldcrest, wren and chaffinch. Most years, small flocks of Scottish crossbills can be heard and sometimes seen as they feed nosily on pine seeds. Capercaillies live in the woods and black grouse display and breed on the moor.

Osprey

Mammals
Red squirrels and roe deer are common, along with foxes, rabbits and hares. On the shores of the loch, otters are seen occasionally.

D Tomlinson

Abernethy Forest Nature Reserve

Insects
Four-spotted chasers, common blue and large red are common dragonflies and in July, Scotch argus butterflies are abundant. In total, 19 species of butterfly and over 260 species of moth have been recorded on the nature reserve. Beetles are also prevalent with over 420 species, some very rare.

Plants
The pinewoods are home to special plants like creeping lady's tresses, lesser twayblade and three species of wintergreens. Altogether, there are 240 plant species on the nature reserve, including 19 sedges.

BEMPTON CLIFFS, HUMBERSIDE

TA/197738 ♿ **I P ♦♦**

Visiting
The nature reserve lies on the B1229 between Flamborough and Filey. Bempton railway station is approximately 2 km (1 mile) from the site. During the summer, boat trips are arranged and leave from Bridlington Harbour to watch birds on the cliffs.

Location and habitat
Bempton, an expanse of cliffs, is one of the best sites to see nesting seabirds on the eastern

mainland of Britain. The cliffs and path extend over 3.6 km (2 miles) and rise to over 130 m (420 ft) from the sea. Five viewpoints are spread on either side of the visitor centre. Rifts have occurred in the chalk cliffs creating ledges, with nooks and crannies that provide excellent nesting sites. The narrow strip of grassland above the cliffs gives the puffins a chance to burrow for their nests. The site also provides a good point for viewing migrants.

M Hamblin

Bempton Cliffs Nature Reserve

Birds

By far the largest colony of seabirds in England is at Bempton. Eight species breed regularly, including the only colony of gannets in England. Puffins can be seen on the upper ledges, while guillemots use open and exposed ledges lower down. Razorbills crowd into crevices and cavities. Both guillemots and razorbills take advantage of open areas to give their young a straight descent to the sea. Kittiwakes are the most numerous bird, which hides the presence of fulmars. However, fulmars can be identified as they glide on the updraughts of wind along the cliffs or glide alongside boats approaching the cliffs, hoping to obtain food. Herring gulls make a disproportionate amount of noise for such a small group, approximately 1,000 pairs compared with 80,000 pairs of kittiwakes. Passing migrants are attracted to Flamborough Head which juts out into the North Sea. Many species turn up at the site in the autumn, including redstarts and both pied and spotted flycatchers. Terns, skuas and shearwaters pass close by in the autumn. Weather permitting, the RSPB organises boat trips from Bridlington Harbour to view these migrants.

Mammals

Grey seals and porpoises are often seen just offshore.

Insects

Up to 15 species of butterfly can be seen, including large, small and green-veined whites and small tortoiseshells. Migrants such as the painted lady and red admiral are seen from midsummer onwards.

Plants

Over 220 species of plant have been recorded from the narrow strip of land between the cliffs and the cultivated fields. The red campion of early summer has a variety of shades from white to deep red. Chalkland plants include common scurvy grass, field mouse-ear, yellow oat and hawkbit.

BLACKTOFT SANDS, HUMBERSIDE

SE/843232 ♿ I P

Visiting

The nature reserve is between Reedness and Ousefleet on the A161. The nearest railway station is Goole, 13 km (8 miles) from the site.

Location and habitat

The reserve sits at the junction of the Rivers Ouse and Trent, on the south side of the Humber. It is one of the largest areas of reedbed in the UK. Five different areas are managed at the nature reserve, with rough grass and saltmarsh, mudflats, lagoons and scrub as well as the reeds. The reeds reach heights of 3 m (9 ft) and shade out most other plants. On higher ground, where the reeds cannot grow, couch grass forms dense swards. Mudflats have formed behind the stone walls at the junction of the two rivers, with the daily overflow from the tides preventing plant growth. Lagoons have been created in the couch grass at the western end of the nature reserve and are screened with willow bushes, alder and elder to provide shelter for smaller birds.

Birds
Bearded tits and reed warblers nest in large numbers in the reedbeds, along with shelducks who take their young to the estuary on the day they hatch. At the edge of the reedbed, sedge and grasshopper warblers, as well as large numbers of reed buntings, make their nests. Ducks such as mallards, teals and gadwalls nest on islands in the lagoons, with other species such as lapwings, snipe, redshanks and little ringed plovers on the islands and around the edges. The willow bushes attract goldfinches, linnets and redpolls to breed. Water levels are lowered in the lagoons in autumn to provide wet mud and shallow water to attract passing waders. Redshanks, greenshanks, wood sandpipers, little stints and curlew sandpipers have all responded to this enticement. Recently, avocets and marsh harriers began nesting and can be seen easily from the hides between April and June.

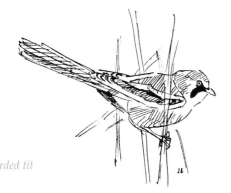

Bearded tit

Insects
Several species of wainscot moth, including the rare fen, silky and crescent striped, exist within the reeds and grasses.

Plants
In addition to the reeds, couch grass forms dense swards. In isolated higher areas, close to the rivers, are edges of saltmarsh where the tides encourage sea clubrush, sea aster and sea purslane to grow.

CONWY, NORTH WALES

SH/800770   ♿ **I P S** ⍟⍟

Visiting
The nature reserve is just off the A55 to the west of Llandudno. By train, Llandudno Junction is on the opposite side of the road from the car park.

Location and habitat
The reserve was formed following the construction of the Conwy tunnel in the 1980s. Since then, we have created reedbeds, lagoons, grassland and estuary habitats. Shallow pools next to the estuary provide ideal feeding and roosting places for ducks, geese and wading birds. The visitor centre allows close views of the birds as well as breathtaking views of Snowdonia and Conwy Castle.

Birds
Many shelducks spend the winter on the estuary and use the nature reserve to feed and bathe. Special shelduck nesting tunnels have been created. The grassland areas have proved very popular for breeding lapwings with more arriving from the Continent in autumn to overwinter. Skylarks sing over the grassland and ringed and little ringed plovers nest on the shingle islands, which also provide roost sites for curlews. Winter species include wigeons and red-breasted mergansers.

Insects
Common blue butterflies can be seen over the grassland, while common darter dragonflies fly the paths.

DUNGENESS, KENT

TR/063196   ♿ **I P** ⍟⍟

Visiting
The nature reserve is off the B2075 Folkestone to Lydd road, with access from the Lydd to Dungeness road, near Boulderwall Farm. Nearest railway station is at Rye, 16 km (10 miles) away.

Sandwich terns

Location and habitat
The nature reserve is on the largest shingle headland in Europe. In 1932, the RSPB established its first nature reserve here to protect shingle-nesting seabirds. Several lagoons, natural and artificial, have been developed to provide further habitats. Altogether, the nature reserve occupies over 850 ha (2,000 acres). Three types of habitat can be found at Dungeness. The large shingle banks formed by the sea provide the basis for the site. Where the shingle meets Romney Marsh, grass and clumps of gorse grow. Several species nest in this area in the spring. The third habitat consists of freshwater lagoons. Islands in the lagoons provide feeding and nesting sites, with vegetation cover for large numbers of migrants.

Birds
The nature reserve is important in the summer for nesting terns and gulls, including Mediterranean gulls and Sandwich terns. In winter, large numbers of surface-feeding ducks are present – mainly mallards, teals and shovelers, but occasionally wigeons, gadwalls and pintails. Wintering diving ducks include tufted ducks, pochards, goldeneyes, goosanders and smews. Dungeness has long been famous as a landfall for birds on migration and every year brings new recordings of unusual species.

Mammals
Most of the small mammals are present, including the pygmy shrew, water shrew and harvest mole.

Reptiles and amphibians
Grass snakes, lizards, marsh frogs and smooth newts are all present in small numbers.

Insects
Migrant butterflies, including peacocks, red admirals and painted ladies, can be seen in summer. Many unusual moths are recorded in late summer and autumn.

Plants
Several unusual plants such as marsh cinquefoil, bulbous meadow-grass, sheep's bit, upright chickweed, Nottingham catchfly and the nationally rare yellow vetch exist at the site.

FAIRBURN INGS, WEST YORKSHIRE

SE/452278   ♿ I P ⚤

Visiting
The nature reserve stretches to the west of the village of Fairburn, which straddles the A1 north of Ferrybridge. The main entrance to the nature reserve is situated half way between Fairburn and the village of Ledston. Castleford is the nearest railway station, 8 km (5 miles) from the western end of the nature reserve.

Location and habitat
Forming part of the industrial section of the Aire Valley, with collieries and a power station, at first sight the area does not appear to be attractive to birds. However, years of coal mining and later disuse have resulted in shallow depressions in the surface and large lakes. Altogether the nature reserve consists of 254 ha (627 acres) of large, shallow lakes, marsh, scrub and floodpools. Trees planted by volunteers, along Fairburn Cut and the riverside, provide nesting sites for many small birds. Reedbeds are also being encouraged. Over

Mute swan

the years, the site has become important for its wildfowl and as a staging post for many migrants.

Birds
Mallards, teals, shovelers and tufted ducks can be seen throughout the year with large flocks of mute swans gathering in the summer to moult and whooper swans arriving to spend the winter. Goldeneyes and goosanders are numerous from November to March and the shallow water and exposed reed attract ruffs, greenshanks and dunlins during spring and autumn. Easterly winds encourage passage birds such as common, arctic and black terns to visit the site on a regular basis. Great crested grebes make floating nests from reeds and sedges, and their young, when very small, can be seen riding on their parents' backs for protection.

Insects
Several species of butterfly are found at the nature reserve. In the spring, small tortoiseshells emerge from winter hibernation. Orange-tips and green-veined whites appear later along with migrants such as red admirals and painted ladies. Warm summer days find the dragonflies and damselflies in hunting mood. Common darters and brown hawkers can be seen along the paths, and blue-tailed damselflies seek their food over the water.

Plants
Silver birch grows well on the slag heaps, and foxgloves and coltsfoot are common.

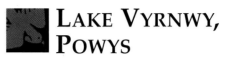 LAKE VYRNWY, POWYS

SJ/016192 ♿ I P S 🚶🚶

Visiting
The nature reserve is 16 km (10 miles) west of Llanfyllin via the B4393 to Llanwddyn. Welshpool is the nearest railway station, 34 km (21 miles) away.

Location and habitat
The nature reserve lies in the Berwyn hills west of Llanfyllin. Lake Vyrnwy reservoir was built at the end of the 19th century. The reservoir is 215 m (700 ft) above sea level, covers 440 ha (1,100 acres) and is up to 20 m (60 ft) deep in places. Around the perimeter of the lake, some of the original plantings of Douglas fir from the turn of the century can still be seen. Originally, the forest consisted of Douglas fir, sitka spruce and Japanese larch and covered over 360 ha (900 acres). Today, about half that area exists. Half the moorland is heather and the remainder,

Lake Vyrnwy Nature Reserve

D Woodfall (Woodfall Wild Images)

grass and bog. It is grazed by Welsh mountain sheep and burnt regularly as part of the moorland management.

Birds

Due to the burning of the moorland and controlled sheep grazing, the area still contains red grouse and breeding curlews and whinchats.

In the woodland, around the lake and in the smaller scrub areas, there are large numbers of garden and willow warblers, blackcaps and chiffchaffs. Pied flycatchers, redstarts and wood warblers frequently burst into song in spring, calling attention to their presence. The younger woods are teeming with breeding birds such as tree pipits and chaffinches. On summer days, buzzards are much in evidence, soaring on the thermals of the valley sides. Ravens produce deep-throated calls, which echo from the high ridges, and on spring nights tawny owls can be heard. On the lake, several pairs of great crested grebes and goosanders thrive along with common sandpipers, mallards and teals. Grey wagtails and dippers are common on the mountain streams and kingfishers can be seen alongside the lake and rivers.

Badger

Mammals

A large badger population exists in the woodland. Polecats and red squirrels are present throughout the forest areas, but are rarely seen. Common species, such as the field vole, provide the birds of prey with an important source of food.

Insects

In shrubby areas, several species of butterfly, including the speckled wood, ringlet, green hairstreak, orange-tip, peacock and some fritillary species, can be found.

Plants

The rich flora of the lower valley bogland includes the graceful, long-stemmed, violet flowers of

butterwort in the summer. The insect-eating sundew is present in early summer. Large areas of fern, such as oak and beech fern, grow along the shaded banks.

LEIGHTON MOSS, LANCASHIRE

SD/478751 &♿ I P S 👫

Visiting

The nature reserve can be reached from the M6 at J35 leading to J35a on the A6. The reserve is opposite Silverdale railway station.

Location and Habitat

Once forming the north-east corner of Morecambe Bay, the area was isolated from the sea by an embankment and tidal sluice. It is now a freshwater marsh fed by several streams that drain the surrounding limestone hills. Open water, reedswamp, fen edge, woodland and scrub all make up the nature reserve. The water is ideal for aquatic plants and is mostly less than a metre (3 ft) deep. Some of the islands in the meres are artificial and consist of rock and soil which were dumped in the shallow water. Other islands have been formed from clumps of iris, cut and then floated to the centres of the mere and staked. Over 80 ha (200 acres) of reed provide one of the most important habitats for bitterns in the UK. The fen edges consist of rush and tussock grass with many willows. The limestone slopes are covered with hawthorn, blackthorn and ash scrub while higher up, the woodland becomes dominated by ash, oak and yew.

Birds

The area represents the most northerly home for breeding bitterns, one of the UK's rarest birds, which, together with bearded tits, reed and sedge warblers, water rails, and reed buntings, make Leighton Moss one of the most important reed habitats in the UK. Marsh harriers breed and are regular spring visitors. Large numbers of pied wagtails and starlings roost in the reeds for most of the year and in spring and autumn swallows and sand martins gather. This abundance of food attracts sparrowhawks and the occasional merlin or hobby. The willow scrub and fen edge encourage grasshopper warblers, redpolls, whitethroats and lesser whitethroats. Black-headed gulls, ducks, coots, moorhens and lapwings breed on the islands. Herons hunt for eels, and swallows, swifts and martins collect insects over the water.

Mammals
A pair of otters has bred in the reedswamp for several years. Red and roe deer are present and the small mammals encourage the birds of prey.

Insects
At the fen edge, many species of moth have been recorded, including the elephant, eyed and poplar hawkmoths. Butterflies include peacocks, tortoiseshells and brimstones. Oaks in the woods hold a good many purple hairstreaks, and on the limestone outcrops and grassy slopes there are pearl-bordered and high brown fritillaries.

Plants
Much of the swamp is dense reed, but there are small areas of yellow flags and reedmace with many willows.

LOCHWINNOCH, STRATHCLYDE

NS/359581 ♿ I P S ♟

Visiting
The nature reserve is situated to the south-west of Glasgow. Lochwinnoch is signposted from the A737. The railway station at Lochwinnoch, with trains from Glasgow Central, is near the entrance to the nature reserve.

Location and habitat
Shallow water and the marshy fringes of Barr Loch and the smaller Aird Meadow, surrounded by deciduous trees provide the nature reserve's main habitats.

Birds
The lochs are major feeding and roosting areas for wildfowl including mallards, tufted ducks, pochards and coots. A wintering flock of up to 500 greylag geese roosts on Barr Loch, together with

whooper swans. Several pairs of great crested grebes use the lochs as a breeding ground and the chances of seeing their elaborate display in spring are good. The marshes around the loch teem with nesting sedge warblers. Reed buntings, a few pairs of grasshopper warblers and water rails can be seen in spring as well. A few hundred pairs of black-headed gulls nest on Aird Meadow. Populations of warblers, finches, thrushes and treecreepers frequent the deciduous trees.

Mammals
Roe deer are seen regularly, and you may be lucky enough to glimpse an otter.

Otter

Plants
The marshes surrounding the lochs are full of reed sweetgrass, canary grass and mountain water sedge. In summer, meadowsweet, valerian, bogbean, flag and purple loosestrife mix with the grass.

MINSMERE, SUFFOLK

TM/452680 ♿ I P S ♟

Visiting
The nature reserve is well signposted from the A12 between Blythburgh and Yoxford. The nearest railway station is at Darsham, 6 km (4 miles) from the site.

Location and habitat
The nature reserve is probably most famous for its success in re-establishing the avocet as a British breeding bird. It occupies some 935 ha (2,311 acres) of reedswamp, grazing marshes, woodland, heath

H Welford

Minsmere Nature Reserve

and arable fields. One section, the Scrape, has wide shallow lagoons which were bulldozed in an area of disused marsh. The nature reserve was extended recently to include neighbouring arable fields which the RSPB plans to restore to heathland. This will benefit nightjars and other species dependent on heath, which was a key habitat of the Suffolk Sandlings – much of which has been lost or destroyed since the Second World War. There is a purpose-built visitor centre with information about the nature reserve.

Birds

The mix of habitats means the nature reserve has a wealth of birds. The Scrape is good for viewing breeding avocets, terns and other waders. Large numbers congregate in late summer and early autumn, displaying a wide variety of plumage. With over 160 ha (400 acres) of reedbed to forage in, bitterns are a breeding species, and marsh harriers, bearded tits and water rails are all regulars. An evening walk along the public footpaths between May and July will produce the

sight and sound of churring nightjars, roding woodcocks, owls, tree pipits and stonechats.

Mammals

Red and muntjac deer occupy the woods during the day, but sometimes can be seen out at night. Otters breed on the nature reserve, though are seldom seen.

Red deer

Insects
Over 300 species of moth, 24 of butterfly, and 66 species of beetle have been counted.

Plants
Common reed dominates the reedbeds, intermingled with small areas of bulrush, pond willow, oak and hawthorn together with marsh sowthistle. Ling, bell heather, gorse and bracken occupy the heath and the woodland is a mixture of oak, Scots pine, sweet chestnut, sycamore, hazel and birch. The small area of pasture contains ragged robin, bog cotton, yellow rattle, various clovers and marsh orchids.

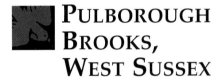 PULBOROUGH BROOKS, WEST SUSSEX

TQ/063165 ♿ I P S ⚲

Visiting
The nature reserve is signposted from the A283 Pulborough to Wiggonholt road. Pulborough railway station is about 3 km (2 miles) from the visitor centre.

Location and habitat
The RSPB has restored this part of the Arun valley to its former glory of wet grassy meadows, making it a haven for wading birds and wildfowl. There are 171 ha (423 acres) of pasture, mixed woods, scrub and bracken. Cattle grazing takes place in the summer on the low-lying areas near the river. Small remnants of woodland, together with hedgerows, provide habitats for a wide range of wildlife.

Birds
In the winter, the brooks are flooded, attracting thousands of ducks including wigeons and pintails, plus a flock of Bewick's swans. When the water level falls in the spring, snipe, redshanks, lapwings and teals breed on the damp meadows. Barn owls can be seen hunting over the nature reserve throughout the year and may be seen via closed circuit TV at the Upperton's Barn visitor centre. Peregrines and merlins can occasionally be seen. The hedgerows provide shelter, nesting and feeding sites for thrushes, tits and warblers. The small amount of woodland sustains nest sites for nuthatches, sparrowhawks and green woodpeckers.

Barn owl

Mammals
Roe and fallow deer and water voles are all present on the site.

Reptiles and fish
Adders and grass snakes are present. Eels in the shallow pools and ditches provide food for grey herons.

Insects
The nationally rare club-tailed dragonfly is one of 19 species counted. Twenty-three butterfly species have also been noted.

RADIPOLE LAKE, DORSET

SY/677796 ♿ I P S ⚲

Visiting
The nature reserve entrance and visitor centre are at the Swannery car park close to the seafront and the railway station in Weymouth.

Location and habitat
Prior to 1924, the lake formed the estuary of the River Wey and was known as the Backwater. Twice daily, saltwater flowed as far as Radipole village until Westham bridge was built, complete with sluices. The tideflow was halted and the area became a freshwater lake. Parts of the lake were colonised by reed after the Second World War. Rubble from houses destroyed by bombing was used to build paths through the reeds, on the southern part of the nature reserve. The rubble came with many garden plants and the paths are now bordered by buddleia and bramble. At the northern end of the nature reserve, water meadows are flanked by dense scrub. The reserve has some 89 ha (219 acres) of open water and reedswamp.

Birds

Many species of wildfowl are present on the lake in winter, including pochards, tufted ducks, wintering gulls, grey herons and teals. Several hundred pied wagtails roost in the reeds as do thousands of starlings. In spring and summer, the reeds are alive with the chattering songs of reed and sedge warblers. The nature reserve is important for bearded tits and Cetti's warblers. Swallows, martins and swifts feed over the water from April to August. Spectacular scenes occur in late summer and early autumn as the birds prepare for migration. Sedge warblers and yellow wagtails collect in hundreds, while swallows, martins and swifts gather in thousands as they prepare for the long journey south.

Mammals

Roe deer and a variety of bats can be seen on the nature reserve.

Reptiles

Grass snakes can be seen.

Insects

With the abundance of buddleia and nettles, butterflies and moths can be found in large numbers, including migrant painted ladies and clouded yellows. The uncommon *Argiope bruennich* spider is also present.

Plants

Yellow flag irises and marsh marigolds are most obvious in the spring. There is a large colony of southern marsh orchids in the pasture area.

Marsh marigold

RYE HOUSE MARSH, HERTFORDSHIRE

TL/386100 ♿ I P

Visiting

The nature reserve is east of Hoddesdon, off the A10, where the site is signposted to Rye Park via Rye road. The nearest railway station is Rye House (on the Liverpool Street line), 300 metres away.

Location and habitat

This well-interpreted site is on Thames Water land and forms part of the Lee Valley Regional Park. It is close to one of the ancient crossing points of the river beside the old Rye House. It's a 19 ha (47 acre) nature reserve of riverside marsh and lagoons containing a variety of habitats including flood meadows, shallow pools and mud, fen, stands of reed and reed sweetgrass, willow and alder scrub and wet woodland.

Birds

In winter, teals, snipe, water rails, green sandpipers, gadwalls and shovelers can be seen. In summer, nesting birds include common waterfowl, reed and sedge warblers, cuckoos and reed buntings. Green and common sandpipers, many swallows, martins and warblers all gather at migration time. From the hides, visitors can have excellent views of kingfishers nesting in artificial sand banks. Nesting rafts have been built on the lagoons for common terns which now breed on the nature reserve. Artificial nest sites for kestrels and sand martins also have breeding birds.

Mammals

Harvest mice and water voles abound and at least five species of bat feed over the nature reserve.

Reptiles

Grass snakes can sometimes be seen.

Plants

Marshland flowers include ragged robin, marsh marigold and water forget-me-not.

SANDWELL VALLEY, BIRMINGHAM

SP/036931 ♿ I P ♟♦

Visiting
The nature reserve is in the heart of the West Midlands off the A4041. From J7 of the M6, follow signs to Sandwell Valley. A left turn into Tanhouse Avenue leads to the nature reserve car park. The nearest railway station is at Hamstead, 1.6 km (1 mile) away.

Goosander

Location and habitat
The nature reserve forms part of Sandwell Valley Country Park and occupies some 10 ha (25 acres). It consists of lake and marsh, with reclaimed grassland. The course of the river and subsidence from the abandoned coal mines produced marsh and wet grassland. A 12 ha (30 acre) lake was constructed between the river and the marsh and the spoil used to landscape the area.

Birds
In winter, a wide variety of waterfowl, including goosanders, gather on the lake with shovelers, teals, snipe and jack snipe occupying the marsh. Closer to the nature centre, redwings and fieldfares feed in the hedgerows with finches and reed buntings visiting the bird feeding station. In spring, wheatears, yellow wagtails and whinchats can be seen as they pass through on migration, while resident birds, such as great crested grebes, mallards, coots and moorhens, begin to nest. The islands and marsh also support breeding lapwings, little ringed plovers and occasionally redshanks. Autumn signals the return of migrants which rest and feed on the lake shore and islands. Dunlins, curlews, greenshanks and common sandpipers have all been recorded.

Insects
Many butterflies can be seen in summer over the grassland, including green-veined whites, small coppers, common blues, and both large and small skippers.

Plants
Around the marsh, water mint, bistort and great burnet are seen. In the grass, red and white campion flourish along with chicory.

SNETTISHAM, NORFOLK

TF/648335 ♿ I P ♟♦

Visiting
The car park for the nature reserve is 3.5 km (2 miles) from Snettisham village and is approached down a narrow lane to the eastern shore of the Wash. The nearest railway station is at King's Lynn, 19 km (12 miles) away.

Location and habitat
The nature reserve extends 3 km (2 miles) south of the car park and consists of a large area of intertidal flats, saltmarsh, brackish lagoons and a shingle beach. At low tide, and on a clear day, the vast expanse of mud provides a spectacular scene with thousands of feeding birds. Similarly, at high tide, thousands of waders make use of the lagoons and beach.

Birds
At first sight, the area might appear devoid of interest for the birdwatcher, and certainly the view across the Wash at low tide, towards the western shore, presents a dull scene. But, at second glance, a magnificent picture comes to light. Over 130,000

Black-tailed godwits

waders roost near the beach and on artificial islands in the winter. Dunlins, knots, bar-tailed godwits, oystercatchers, redshanks, curlews, turnstones and ringed plovers are all included. Thousands of pink-footed and brent geese, together with ducks including shelducks, mallards, wigeons, pintails and teals, use the foreshore for feeding and roosting. And in the summer, the pits have a nesting colony of common terns. Dozens of redshanks, skylarks, meadow pipits and reed buntings breed on the saltmarsh and many pairs of breeding waterfowl occur in the water-filled shingle pits.

South Stack Cliffs Nature Reserve

D Broadbent (RSPB Images)

Mammals
Rabbits predominate and can easily be seen around the hides.

Plants
Shingle beach flora include yellow horned poppy, sea beet and hoary mullein.

SOUTH STACK CLIFFS, ANGLESEY

SH/210818 ♿ **I P** 👫

Visiting
Ellin's Tower and the nature reserve are signposted from Holyhead. The railway station at Holyhead is 5.6 km (3.5 miles) from the nature reserve.

Location and habitat
The western headland of Anglesey provides the birdwatcher with one of the most spectacular scenes in the British Isles. Magnificent cliffs, eroded by centuries of weather, rise from the sea to over 120 m (400 ft). The ledges and caves provide ideal nesting sites for seabirds. Further enhancement of the scene is provided by the white sandstone of Holyhead Mountain, particularly when covered with purple heather. To the south, Penrhos Feilw Common is rich in plant life, with heather and gorse of a type that once covered much of the south-west coast of Britain.

Birds
From April to July, the ledges are crowded with nesting guillemots, razorbills and puffins. A kittiwake colony, to the south of the lighthouse, can also be seen at this time. Views of the cliffs and birds can be seen from Ellin's Tower, although a walk down the pathway to the lighthouse can prove fruitful in fine weather. The Tower also provides live TV pictures of the breeding seabirds. Choughs nest in the caves and are often seen over the cliff-top sward searching for insects. The slopes of the mountain behind the cliffs hold many stonechats, and the gorse provides nesting sites for whitethroats and shelter for resting migrants. Lapwings and redshanks nest on Penrhos Feilw. Waders, such as whimbrels, greenshanks and dotterels, pause on migration. Harriers and short-eared owls on passage hunt over the common.

Reptiles
Adders and lizards can sometimes be seen basking in the sun.

Insects
On the warm days of summer, dozens of silver-studded blue butterflies, small pearl-bordered fritillaries, graylings and gatekeepers appear.

Plants
The spring brings a variety of blooms to the cliff-top, including spring squill, thrift, sea campion,

and the rare and unusual spathulate fleawort. Early summer finds the mountain dotted with hundreds of heath spotted orchids. The nature reserve's rarest plant, the spotted rock rose, grows in a few small colonies. The heathland is dominated by four plants: ling, bell heather, cross-leaved heath and dwarf gorse.

TITCHWELL MARSH, NORFOLK

TF/749436 ♿ I P S ♟♟

Visiting
The nature reserve is 9.6 km (6 miles) east of Hunstanton between the A149 road to Brancaster and the sea. The nearest railway station is at King's Lynn 37 km (23 miles) from the nature reserve. During the summer, buses from Hunstanton will stop at Titchwell.

Location and habitat
Saltmarsh covers the largest section of the nature reserve. Prior to 1954, it did not exist at all, and farming, both beef and root crops, took place. The sea defences were breached in 1953 which allowed the tides to ebb and flow over the previously well-drained farmland. Banks of sand and shingle formed on both sides of the breach and have gradually increased in height and area. On the southern edge of the saltmarsh, an extensive reedbed has formed and is subject to tidal flooding. The completion of a seawall in 1979 created the freshwater and brackish marshes which improved the site for breeding and non-breeding birds. The shallow lagoons contain large numbers of ragworms, mud shrimps, sticklebacks and fly larvae, which provide food for many birds. Water levels are controlled to produce ideal conditions for feeding and nesting birds. The freshwater reeds, growing in standing water, support many insects, eels and toads.

Birds
The main shingle area is colonised by little and common terns, oystercatchers and ringed plovers. Many knots and godwits roost when the Wash is flooded with equinox tides. Dunlins, curlews, sandpipers, greenshanks and other waders feed on the lagoons in autumn. Goldeneyes, mergansers, little grebes and brent geese occur in winter. Several hundred pairs of black-headed gulls nest on the lagoon islands, together with coots, little grebes, shovelers, tufted ducks and gadwalls. Hundreds of martins, swallows and swifts feed on the insects over the water in autumn. Marsh harriers and bearded tits nest in the reedbed, as do reed warblers and reed buntings. Bitterns are frequent visitors.

Plants
Sea sandwort, sea couch grass and prickly saltwort grow in the higher areas of the sand and shingle. Sea lavender is abundant on the adjacent Thornham Marsh.

VANE FARM, PERTH AND KINROSS

NT/160991 ♿ I P S ♟♟

Visiting
The nature reserve is signposted from the M90 and is only half-an-hour's drive from Edinburgh. The nearest railway station is at Cowdenbeath 13 km (8 miles) away.

Location and habitat
This is one of the most popular RSPB nature reserves in Scotland. It is next to the National Nature Reserve at Loch Leven and is famous for its panoramic views stretching from the loch shore to the top of the Vane (Hill) which rises over 250 m (820 ft). A variety of habitats surround this educational nature centre including open water, wet and dry grassland, birch and mixed woodland and heather moorland with rocky outcrops. A roomy reception hide gives excellent close views of

Common toad

a variety of loch shore birds and two trails allow visitors a beautiful walk in the birch woodland and heather moor.

Birds
The nature reserve is renowned for pink-footed geese, with up to 23,000 arriving in autumn. Whooper swans, greylag geese, wigeons, teals, mallards and pintails also visit during the winter. The woodlands have both tawny and long-eared owls, green and great spotted woodpeckers, tree pipits, spotted flycatchers and willow warblers. Great crested and little grebes, shelducks, gadwalls, shovelers and tufted ducks nest by the lagoons and the wet grassland areas provide nesting habitat for lapwings, oystercatchers, curlews, snipe and redshanks.

Other wildlife
Over 250 species of plants have been recorded. Roe deer, water voles and foxes are seen regularly.

YNYS-HIR, DYFED

SN/686956 ♿ I P ♟♟

Visiting
The nature reserve car park is reached from the A487 between Machynlleth and Aberystwyth at the village of Eglwys-fach. The nearest railway station is Machynlleth, 10 km (6 miles) away, from where there are regular buses.

Location and habitat
The nature reserve is situated on the Dyfi Estuary and consists of an exciting range of habitats, including sessile oak woodland, reedbeds, freshwater pools and saltmarshes.

Birds
At Foel Fawr, wheatears, stonechats, whinchats, tree pipits and yellowhammers nest among the rocks. Spring is the best time to visit the woodland, when the birds are in full song. Tits, finches, warblers, thrushes, pied flycatchers, redstarts and all three woodpeckers breed. Buzzards circle overhead and tawny owls can also be seen.

Buzzard

Dippers, grey wagtails, common sandpipers and red-breasted mergansers can be seen on the river and freshwater pools. Wigeons and Greenland white-fronted geese spend the winter on the estuary, together with large flocks of curlews and oystercatchers. Sightings of peregrines, sparrowhawks, red kites and buzzards are frequent. Kingfishers, which sometimes breed, move down to the estuary in late summer.

Mammals
Polecats, dormice and otters are resident, but are difficult to see.

Insects
Butterflies include the green hairstreak, grayling and three kinds of fritillary. Several species of moth have been recorded, including the emperor, fox and northern eggar.

Grayling

Plants
At sea level, the bogs have important numbers of dragonflies and locally scarce plants including all three sundew species.

ENGLAND

SOUTH-EAST

Adur Estuary, West Sussex

TQ/211050

The 10 ha (24 acres) of intertidal mudflats and saltmarsh attract birds such as greenshanks, ringed plovers, bar-tailed godwits and several species of gull. Sea purslane, glasswort and sea aster are some of the saltwater plants.

Blean Woods, Kent

TR/126593 ♿ I P

One of the largest areas of ancient broadleaved woodland in southern England, the nature reserve is a patchwork of different habitats providing a variety of sights and sounds for visitors. The wood is a mixture of oaks, birches and sweet chestnuts providing plenty of seeds and insects for birds such as woodpeckers, tits, nuthatches and treecreepers. There are large areas of coppice, allowing flowers like the yellow-flowered cow-wheat to grow. This is the food plant for the caterpillars of the rare heath fritillary butterfly. The heath, which was created in the 1980s, attracts tree pipits and nightjars.

Elmley Marshes, Kent

TQ/926705 I P ⛺

The wet grassland of Elmley Marshes attracts thousands of ducks, geese and wading birds in the winter. Hen harriers, merlins, peregrines and short-eared owls can also be seen during the winter. In the summer, many wading birds, including the elegant avocet, breed on the nature reserve.

Short-eared owl

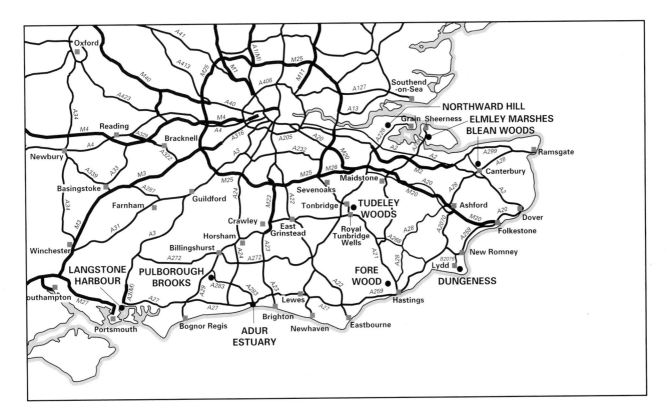

Fore Wood, East Sussex

TQ/756126 P

This undulating woodland of hornbeam, chestnut and oak with two ravine streams running through it, has breeding great, marsh and willow tits. You can also see or hear woodpeckers, nightingales and warblers. Bluebells, wood anemones and early purple orchids are abundant in the spring.

Langstone Harbour, Hampshire

SU/718029 P

The entire harbour, with its mudflats, saltmarsh and shingle islands, is outstanding for wintering wildfowl including thousands of brent geese. Wigeons, teals, oystercatchers, common terns, grebes and greenshanks occur regularly throughout the breeding season.

Turtle doves

Northward Hill, Kent

TQ/784759 P

Northward Hill is an excellent woodland for birds. As well as nightingales and turtle doves, the wood has the largest heronry in the UK, with over 200 pairs of grey herons nesting in the treetops. There is also a large area of grazing marsh, where wading birds breed and wildfowl spend the winter.

Tudeley Woods, Kent

TQ/618434 P

All three British species of woodpecker live in the wood, as well as nuthatches and treecreepers. The springtime carpet of bluebells and primroses is an impressive sight. This is also a good time to listen to the songs of the many different warblers that nest on the nature reserve. In the summer, look out for orchids and butterflies, including the white admiral and speckled wood.

SOUTH-WEST

Arne, Dorset

SY/473882 I P ♟♟

Arne is one of the finest examples of maritime-influenced lowland heath and valley mire systems in the UK. The nature reserve also holds extensive areas of saltmarsh that lead on to the mudflats of Poole Harbour. A nature trail covers most of the reserve habitats. Nationally important breeding populations of Dartford warblers and nightjars, and internationally important populations of passage or wintering shelducks, red-breasted mergansers and black-tailed godwits are found. All six species of British reptile, the nationally scarce Dorset heath (*Erica ciliaris*), 23 species of dragonfly and roe and sika deer may also be seen.

Aylesbeare Common, Devon

SY/057898 P

A 1,100 ha (2,700 acre) series of southern heathland commons, including this nature reserve, forms part of the internationally important East Devon Pebblebed heaths. It is an important habitat for Dartford warblers, nightjars, stonechats and other heathland birds, and yellowhammers, linnets and both meadow and tree pipits abound. Thirty-six species of butterfly have been seen on the nature reserve since 1976. The wetter areas are home to numerous dragon and damselflies which include the internationally endangered southern damselfly among the 24 species so far found on the reserve. In late summer, the yellow flowering western gorse really sets off the purple of the heathers.

Chapel Wood, Devon

SS/483413

This is a small but varied area of mainly deciduous woodland. Situated on a hillside, the highest area contains the remains of an old hill fort; the chapel and well (both registered monuments) are beside the stream. A good number of woodland birds can be seen, including pied flycatchers, wood warblers and all three woodpeckers. Twenty-five species of butterfly have been recorded. Dragonflies, badgers, bluebells and primroses can also be seen at various times of the year.

Exe Estuary Reserves, Devon:

Bowling Green Marsh
SX/968881 ♿

Exminster Marshes
SX/954872 **P**

These coastal grazing marshes lie either side of the Exe Estuary and contain a range of habitats, including freshwater ditches and pools, noted for their wide variety of plants. Flooding in winter attracts large numbers of estuary birds including curlews, black-tailed godwits and wigeons. Both sites act as high tide roosts, holding important numbers of passage waders such as greenshanks and whimbrels. Breeding birds include lapwings and redshanks on the open fields, buzzards and ravens in nearby trees and Cetti's, reed and sedge warblers along the road and scrub of the canal banks.

Garston Wood, Dorset
SU/004194 **P**

This is a 34 ha (84 acre), semi-natural, ancient coppice woodland, managed on a 10 year coppice cycle. Seven hectares (17 acres) have been left to develop into high forest woodland with many oak and ash standards. Botanically very interesting, over 200 species of plants have been recorded, of which many, such as the bluebell, wood anemone and primrose, are ancient woodland species. April/May is the best time for the flowering spectacle. Forty-one bird species have bred, including the nightingale and turtle dove. Twenty-nine species of butterfly have been recorded including fritillaries and white admirals. Dormice, badgers and fallow deer are also present.

Great spotted woodpecker

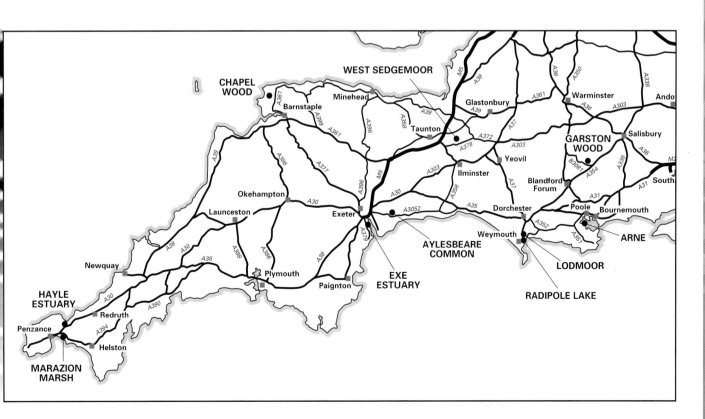

Hayle Estuary, Cornwall

SW/546364 ♿

Situated 9 km (5.5 miles) north-east of Penzance and 4 km (2.5 miles) south-east of St Ives, this is a small, compact estuary in the town of Hayle opening into St Ives Bay. It is of particular importance in cold weather, when up to 18,000 birds are recorded including wigeons, teals, shelducks, curlews, dunlins and golden plovers. North American vagrants include ring-billed gulls at Copperhouse Creek car parks. Great northern divers, red-necked grebes and goldeneyes regularly occur in winter; passage terns and waders appear in spring and autumn.

Lodmoor, Dorset

SY/686807 ♿ **P** 👫

Grazing marsh, with dykes, shallow pools, reedbeds and scrub make up Lodmoor Nature Reserve. In the summer, the reedbeds have breeding reed warblers, bearded tits and reed buntings. Where the reedbeds merge into scrub, both Cetti's and sedge warblers can be found. Mallards, shovelers, shelducks and yellow wagtails breed out on the moor itself. There are many passage migrants during the spring and autumn, including large numbers of martins and swallows. A variety of waders, such as greenshanks, redshanks, common and green sandpipers, use the pools to feed. Both the common spotted and bee orchid are seen in spring, whereas late summer is the best time to see the flowering sea aster. In the winter months, gadwalls, mallards, shovelers, teals and wigeons are present, and there are large numbers of golden plovers and lapwings out on the moor.

Marazion Marsh, Cornwall

SW/513311 P

Situated on the south coast at Mount's Bay, almost opposite St Michael's Mount, the marsh constitutes the largest area of reedbed in the county and has numerous shallow, freshwater pools. Grey herons, mallards, coots, moorhens, sedge, reed and Cetti's warblers breed. The nature reserve is particularly good in summer for dragonflies and plants and for passage aquatic warblers and spotted crakes in August-September.

West Sedgemoor, Somerset

ST/361238 ♿ **I P**

The nature reserve is part of the Somerset Levels and Moors, an area of low-lying wet meadows covering 526 ha (1,300 acres), bordered by deciduous woodland. Winter flooding dries in spring to allow cattle grazing and hay cutting in the summer months. Breeding birds on the moor include lapwings, snipe, curlews, redshanks and quails, while one of Britain's largest heronries, of about 90 pairs, can be viewed in Swell Wood (a hide has wheelchair access from the car park). Winter flooding attracts large and often spectacular flocks of waterfowl to the moor, especially teals, wigeons, lapwings and golden plovers. Meadow flora includes marsh marigold, ragged robin and southern marsh orchid. Roe deer and brown hare are often seen.

CENTRAL ENGLAND

Church Wood, Buckinghamshire

SU/968873 P

This small mixed woodland has a remarkable variety of trees and shrubs. These are predominantly oak, beech, field maple and ash with an understorey of hazel, holly, birch, bramble and bracken. The woodland supports a wide variety of breeding birds, including all three species of woodpecker, nuthatches, treecreepers, blackcaps, garden warblers, willow warblers, chiffchaffs, woodcocks and sparrowhawks. In spring, the woodland resounds to the song of all of the woodland species and the woodland floor is carpeted with bluebells, primroses and wood anemones. It also supports a large butterfly population with over 20 species recorded, including the white admiral, purple hairstreak, brimstone and orange tip.

Treecreeper

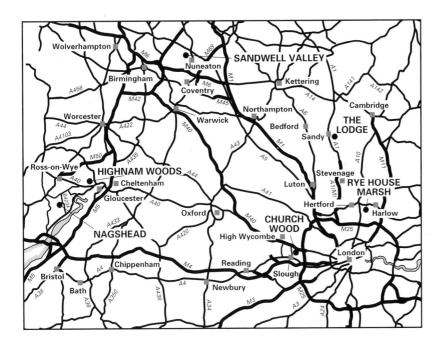

blackcaps and garden warblers all breed on the nature reserve. Muntjac deer and foxes can also be seen.

Nagshead, Gloucestershire

SO/610090

Nagshead is a woodland reserve in the heart of the Forest of Dean. It covers 308 ha (761 acres) of which 176 ha (434 acres) are mature oak woodland and the remainder is younger woodland of various types. Pied flycatchers, wood warblers, redstarts, hawfinches and buzzards can all be seen. A nestbox scheme on the nature reserve has been monitored every year since 1948, making it one of the longest monitored schemes anywhere in the world. Thirty-five species of butterfly have been recorded, including the silver-washed fritillary and white admiral. Dragonflies and damselflies frequent the nature reserve's streams and pools, and fungi are numerous in the autumn.

EAST ANGLIA

Berney Marshes and Breydon Water, Norfolk

TG/465055

Berney is 277 ha (684 acres) of lowland wet grassland set in a remote corner of the Halvergate Marshes. A network of ditches crosses the grazing marshes which are flooded from late autumn to early summer, attracting Bewick's swan, white-fronted geese, wigeons, teals and, in spring, nesting avocets. The nature reserve supports a thriving population of brown hares. The nearby estuary, Breydon Water, has easier access. Breydon has been a nature reserve since 1888. Many rare birds have been recorded here, especially migrant waders. More predictable are wintering golden plovers, pintails, curlews and redshanks. There is a regionally important colony of common terns.

Highnam Woods, Gloucestershire

SO/778190 ♿ P

Covering over 119 ha (294 acres), this broadleaved woodland is dominated by oak and ash, and supports a wide variety of trees including the scarce wild service tree. Highnam Woods provides habitats for a wide variety of woodland birds including all three species of woodpecker, sparrowhawks and tawny owls. Other birds include buzzards and grasshopper warblers, but the nature reserve is best known for its population of nightingales. A bird feeding station (Oct-March) gives good views of many woodland birds. Carpets of bluebells and other spring flowers make the nature reserve particularly attractive in spring. Foxes and badgers may be glimpsed while white admiral and white-letter hairstreak are two of the scarcer species among a rich butterfly community.

The Lodge, Bedfordshire

TL/192486 ♿ I P ⚦

The Lodge Nature Reserve is home of the RSPB's UK headquarters. Perched on the Greensand Ridge, it covers 43 ha (106 acres) of mature woodland, pine plantations, birch and bracken slopes with a remnant heath. Formal gardens adjoin the Victorian mansion. Green and great spotted woodpeckers, nuthatches, treecreepers,

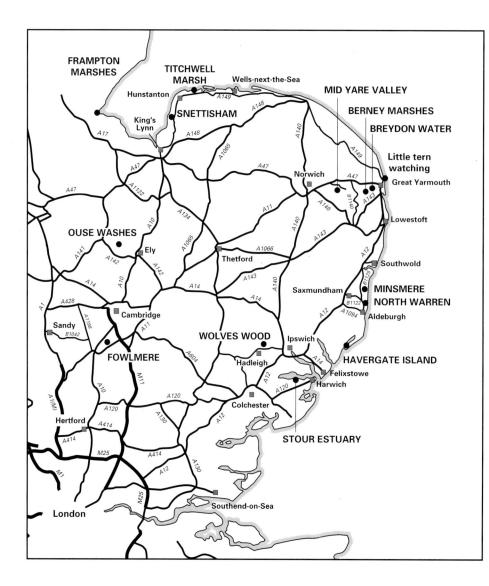

Fowlmere, Cambridgeshire

TL/407461 ♿ I P

Natural springs bubble up from the underlying chalk to irrigate a wetland oasis in an area of well-drained agricultural land. Kingfishers find the nature reserve's many pools and ditches good hunting grounds, and are frequently seen. Other specialities include water rails, turtle doves and a variety of warblers including reed, sedge and grasshopper warblers – all of which breed in the extensive reedbeds. Rare visitors have included wintering bitterns and passage spotted crakes. With luck, you may encounter a grass snake basking beside the trail. Toads can be abundant in spring. Colourful flowers such as the southern marsh orchid, cowslip and hemp agrimony catch the eye in spring and summer, attracting butterflies such as the brimstone and common blue.

Buckenham and Cantley Marshes, Norfolk (part of Mid Yare Valley Nature Reserve)

TG/355050 TG/373038 ♿ P

This area of lowland wet grassland is of national importance as England's only regular wintering site for bean geese (late November-February). White-fronted geese also spend the winter, as do wigeons, occasionally in internationally important numbers. The site also supports breeding marsh harriers, waders, barn owls, passage waders, a variety of dragonflies and a rich flora both in the dykes and on some of the meadows.

Frampton Marshes, Lincolnshire

TF/355394 I P

One of the oldest and most extensive areas of saltmarsh on the Wash, this nature reserve perhaps looks its best during late summer when large areas are carpeted with sea lavender and sea aster. During the winter, large numbers of brent geese graze the saltmarsh. By the time they leave in May, up to 300 pairs of redshanks are well into their noisy breeding cycle. Marsh harriers can be seen throughout the spring and summer, giving way to hen harriers, merlins and short-eared owls in winter.

Havergate Island, Suffolk
TM/415475 I 🚹🚹

The nature reserve is mainly shallow coastal lagoons with low nesting islands. Most of the island is fringed with saltmarsh that is now an important habitat in its own right. Havergate Island is important for its large number of nesting and wintering avocets. Most years, around 150–200 pairs of Sandwich terns also nest. Common terns are among other species which nest on the nature reserve. Large numbers of wintering duck species use the island as a refuge. During the summer, the saltmarsh is a picture of colour with thrift and sea lavender. The shingle ridge to the south of the island supports plants such as herb Robert, sea campion, yellow and English stonecrop and yellow vetch.

North Warren and Aldringham Walks, Suffolk
TM/467575 I P

The nature reserve includes an extensive area of coastal grazing marsh important for breeding waders, particularly lapwings and redshanks. Wintering wildfowl include large flocks of Bewick's swans, white-fronted geese, wigeons, gadwalls, teals and shovelers. A wide variety of waders occur on migration, particularly spotted redshanks, black-tailed godwits and wood sandpipers. The 11 kilometres of dykes support 18 species of dragonflies and rare plants such as brackish-water crowfoot and greater spearwort. The Sandlings heathland attracts good numbers of breeding nightjars, woodlarks and tree pipits plus grayling and green hairstreak butterflies. Otters, bitterns and bearded tits occur in the reedbeds, while the woodlands support turtle doves, nightingales and a host of breeding warblers.

Ouse Washes, Cambridgeshire
TL/471861 ♿ I P 🚹🚹

This extensive area of wet meadowland is dissected by numerous ditches and contained by two parallel

Teal

rivers. In summer, it is one of the best areas for breeding waders in Britain. Around 900 pairs of waders breed – redshanks, lapwings, snipe and black-tailed godwits. Spotted crakes, garganeys, shovelers, gadwalls and yellow wagtails also breed. Many species of dragonfly, including the scarce chaser, hunt along the rivers and ditches. Nearly half of the British aquatic plants have been recorded. During winter floods, this is the most important inland site in Britain for waterfowl. Some 5,000 Bewick's and over 1,000 whooper swans are present regularly. Important numbers of wigeons, teals, mallards, shovelers and pintails also winter here. Ruffs and black-tailed godwits pass through in good numbers in spring.

Stour Estuary, Essex
TM/189309 P

This nature reserve comprises an area of sweet chestnut coppice, grading into saltmarsh and vast expanses of intertidal mudflats. It is the only place in Essex where woodland tumbles into the sea. Of particular importance for wintering waders and wildfowl, there are good populations of black-tailed godwits, dunlins, grey plovers, pintails and brent geese. In summer, the flower-rich woodlands and meadows support a good range of breeding migratory warblers, all three species of woodpecker and nightingales. Occasional sparrowhawks may be glimpsed hunting along the woodland rides, or in winter over the saltmarsh wader roost. There are 25 butterfly species including the white admiral at its only Essex station. The varied plant life includes butcher's broom, the wild service tree and a sea of wood anemones in the spring.

Strumpshaw Fen, Norfolk (part of Mid Yare Valley Nature Reserve)
TG/341066 ♿ **I P** 👫

The nature reserve covers an area of reed fen and open water with willow and alder carr, fen meadows and mixed woodland. It is important for breeding marsh harriers, bearded tits and Cetti's warblers. Bitterns occur regularly and are potential breeders in the near future. The grassland supports breeding waders and is botanically very rich; the flower meadows are open from late June to September. In addition, the site supports healthy populations of swallowtail butterflies and Norfolk hawker dragonflies. It is also possible to see Chinese water deer, particularly at dusk when barn owls also regularly quarter the meadows.

Snipe

Surlingham Church Marsh, Norfolk (part of Mid Yare Valley Nature Reserve)
TG/306065 P

This is a good example of a range of Broadland habitats, with shallow scrapes, dykes, mown fen and reedbeds. There are two hides overlooking this 28 ha (68 acre) nature reserve, accessed by a perimeter footpath (this may be difficult at times due to flooding). There are breeding marsh harriers, snipe, lapwings and redshanks, reed and Cetti's warblers and shovelers. Passage waders include greenshanks and green sandpipers. During the winter, there are large wildfowl roosts and sometimes hen harriers and bearded tits. The site also has many plants, including marsh orchids and bogbeans. Dragonflies hunt the dykes and Chinese water deer are seen regularly.

Tetney Marshes, Lincolnshire
TA/345025 (see map on page 120)

Over 1,000 ha (2,465 acres) of sandflats bordered by low sand dunes and a wide saltmarsh make up Tetney Marshes. Little terns nest at the tide's edge; shelducks, oystercatchers, ringed plovers and redshanks also breed. Wigeons, teals, oystercatchers and golden plovers flock in winter. You may be lucky enough to glimpse a grey seal.

Wolves Wood, Suffolk
TM/054436 I P

This is a very attractive woodland, noted both for its ponds and large range of tree and scrub species, including an extensive area of hornbeam coppice. The coppice is attractive to the hawfinch, a species that breeds in the wood from time to time. Flowering plants include the locally scarce herb Paris, a range of orchid species including the violet helleborine, and patches of bugle and yellow archangel. Spring is the best time to visit the nature reserve when nightingales are much in evidence and late evening visits afford the lucky observer the chance of seeing a 'roding' woodcock. Nuthatches also breed, along with lesser spotted woodpeckers and treecreepers. Recently cut coppice supports a varied range of breeding migratory warblers and butterfly species including good numbers of Essex and little skippers.

Hawfinch

NORTH-WEST

Churnet Valley Woods, Staffordshire
SJ/990489 P

This nature reserve of ancient woodland is important for plants, including early purple orchid and climbing cordalis, and insects, as well as woodpeckers, nuthatches, sparrowhawks and whitethroats. The wood supports badgers and foxes and the stream is one of the few remaining sites for the freshwater crayfish.

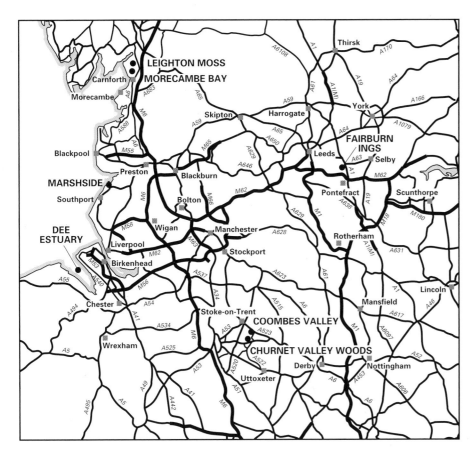

important saltmarsh moths and several species of bat have been recorded.

Marshside, Merseyside

SD/352204

Marshside comprises 110 ha (273 acres) of coastal grazing marsh on the edge of Southport, adjacent to the Ribble Estuary. Cattle graze the grassland in summer, which benefits nesting birds such as lapwings, snipe and redshanks and attracts large numbers of wintering birds. Pink-footed geese, wigeons, golden plovers and teals are common, while smaller numbers of ruffs, black-tailed godwits and pink-footed geese may be seen. Birdwatching is easy from the road along the seawall.

Coombes Valley, Staffordshire

SK/009534 I P ♠♠

Most of the nature reserve consists of mature woodland, mainly oak and birch and some mountain ash and holly. Coombes Brook supports grey wagtails and dippers, while in summer, redstarts and pied flycatchers may be viewed from the tree-hide. Tawny owls, long-eared owls, goshawks and badgers are also present. The nature reserve is especially important for its populations of dead-wood invertebrates.

Dee Estuary, Gayton Sands, Cheshire

SJ/274789 P

The nature reserve is a huge area of intertidal saltmarsh, largely of cord-grass with many brackish pools. These support feeding redshanks, teals and black-tailed godwits, while shelducks and oystercatchers are colourful residents. On particular high tides, large winter flocks of waders such as grey plovers, dunlins, curlews and knots may be seen. The nature reserve supports

Morecambe Bay, Lancashire

SD/468666 ♿ P

This large expanse of intertidal mud and sand with fringing saltmarshes is especially important in winter for vast flocks of waders and wildfowl, including dunlins, knots, oystercatchers, redshanks, bar-tailed godwits, pintails, red-breasted mergansers and greylag geese. The estuary supports important populations of mud-dwelling invertebrates and several rare plants, eg petty spurge and sea radish.

Knot

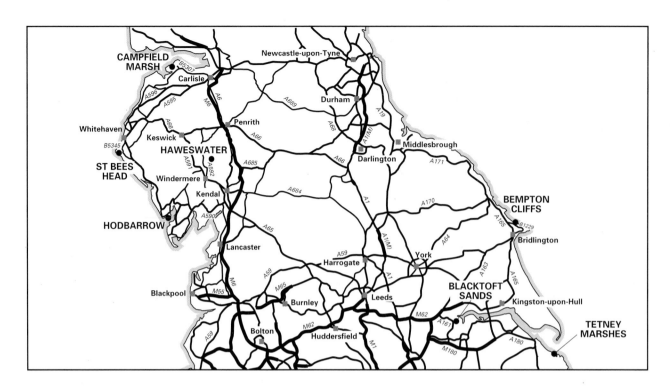

North England

Campfield Marsh, Cumbria
NY/207620 and NY/195616 P

This is beside one of the largest areas of lowland raised mires in England. At high tide, the saltmarsh supports the largest wader roosts on the Solway Estuary with oystercatchers, knots, curlews and grey plovers among them. Peregrines, merlins and barn owls are often seen hunting and in late winter pink-footed geese re-fuel before leaving for Iceland. The typical saltmarsh flora is enhanced by northern marsh orchids while on the mire, sundews, bog rosemary and spotted orchids can be seen along with adders, large heath butterflies and roe deer.

Haweswater, Cumbria
NY/480140 P

An area of mountains, grassland and woodland surround the Haweswater reservoir. Typical western woodland birds such as pied flycatchers, wood warblers and redstarts abound in the spring. Wheatears and ring ouzels frequent the open fell along with peregrines, ravens and England's only breeding pair of golden eagles. The area is rich in ferns and mosses with a diverse flora including primroses, bluebells and sundews.

Hodbarrow, Cumbria
SD/174791 P

This quiet coastal nature reserve has a level path around a brackish lagoon bordered by scrub and grassland. A hide overlooks the tern island and wader roost and also provides excellent views of the many wildfowl species that use the nature reserve. The rare natterjack toad breeds in shallow pools and several orchid species flower in the limestone grassland.

St Bees Head, Cumbria
NX/962118 P ⛷⛷

Three miles of sandstone cliffs, up to 90 m (300 ft) high, hold the largest seabird colony on the west coast of England. Razorbills, guillemots, kittiwakes, a small number of puffins and the only black guillemots breeding in England, can be seen from the four viewpoints near the lighthouse. The walk to the viewpoints is long and steep in parts, but a good variety of plant life, including rock samphire, bloody cranesbill and heath spotted orchid, can be seen on the way.

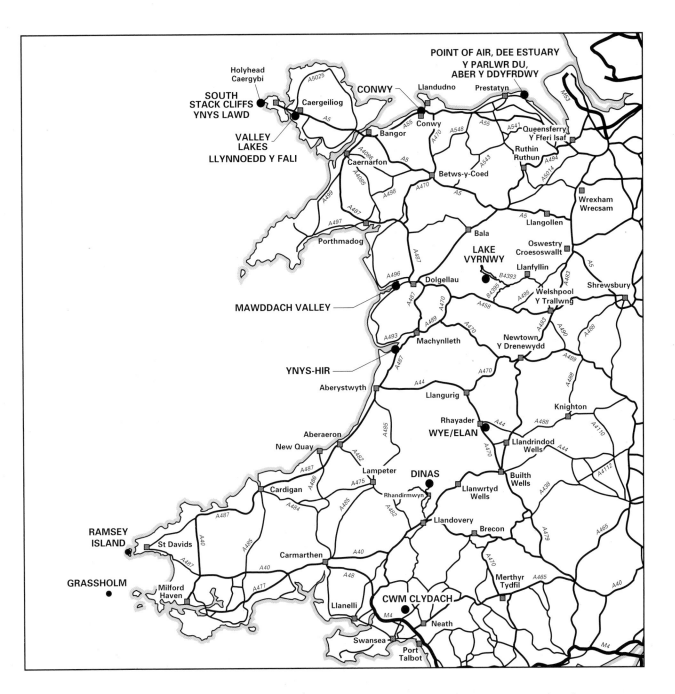

 # WALES

Cwm Clydach, West Glamorgan

SN/682053 P

Lying on the bank of the River Clydach, this oak woodland provides a nesting haven for buzzards, sparrowhawks, pied flycatchers, woodpeckers, warblers, treecreepers and tawny owls, to name but a few. Badgers and foxes frequent the nature reserve, along with many species of butterflies.

Point of Air, Dee Estuary, Clwyd

SJ/113833 P

As this nature reserve overlooks the Dee Estuary, it is a great place to watch estuary birds. It is at its best in the winter when thousands of wading birds and wildfowl feed on the mudflats. When the tide rises, the birds are forced onto the saltmarshes, giving even closer views.

Dinas, Dyfed
SN/788472 **I P**
The 45 ha (111 acre) Dinas woodland clothes the slopes of a steep, conical hill and was once home to breeding red kites. Now it is home in summer to a large population of pied flycatchers, wood warblers and redstarts. Kites are still seen frequently, along with ravens, buzzards, peregrines and sparrowhawks. The River Tywi, which bounds the nature reserve on two sides, supports breeding dippers, common sandpipers and goosanders.

Wye/Elan, Powys
SN/980672 **P**
The 420 ha (1,037 acre) Wye and Elan Valleys Nature Reserve comprises heather moorland, deciduous woodlands, pastures, mires and hay meadows. The Dyffryn woodland is oak and supports breeding redstarts, pied flycatchers and wood warblers. The hillside above the woodland is frequented by red kites, peregrines, whinchats and ravens. There are spectacular views over the Wye Valley and the Cambrian mountain plateau.

Grassholm, Dyfed
SM/599093 (Remote island) **I**
This tiny nine hectare (22 acre) nature reserve is a flat-topped lump of whitewashed basalt, 16 km (10 miles) off the tip of west Wales. Between February and October, it holds 33,000 pairs of breeding gannets. Smaller numbers of guillemots, shags, kittiwakes and three species of larger gull nest round the edge of the gannet colony. Porpoises and dolphins may be seen on the trip out and seals often haul out on the island rocks. The nature reserve is reached only in good weather after a one-hour boat trip from either Martinshaven, Marloes or Whitesands Bay, St David's.

Mawddach Valley, Gwynedd
AS/687191
This nature reserve is situated in the superb scenery of the Mawddach Valley and offers beautiful walks through oak woodland. In the spring, pied flycatchers, wood warblers and redstarts can be seen and heard in the wood. Ravens and buzzards can be seen all year round.

Ramsey Island, Dyfed
SM/702240 **I** 🏃🏃
The 253 ha (625 acre) island nature reserve is a stronghold for the chough, a rare member of the crow family. Guillemots, razorbills and kittiwakes breed on the high western cliffs in summer, and Manx shearwaters nest in the rabbit-grazed cliff-slopes. Wheatears, lapwings and skylarks soar and tumble over the central fields, while ravens, peregrines, buzzards and kestrels patrol the coast. Sea pink, spring squill and sea campion provide plenty of spring colour, and the maritime heath flowers purple and gold in late summer. In autumn, grey seals arrive to pup on the rocky beaches.

Valley Lakes, Gwynedd
SH/315766 **P**
Around this small nature reserve, you will find reed-fringed lakes and small rock outcrops. A variety of ducks and other waterfowl can be seen.

Ramsey Island Nature Reserve

C H Gomersall (RSPB Images)

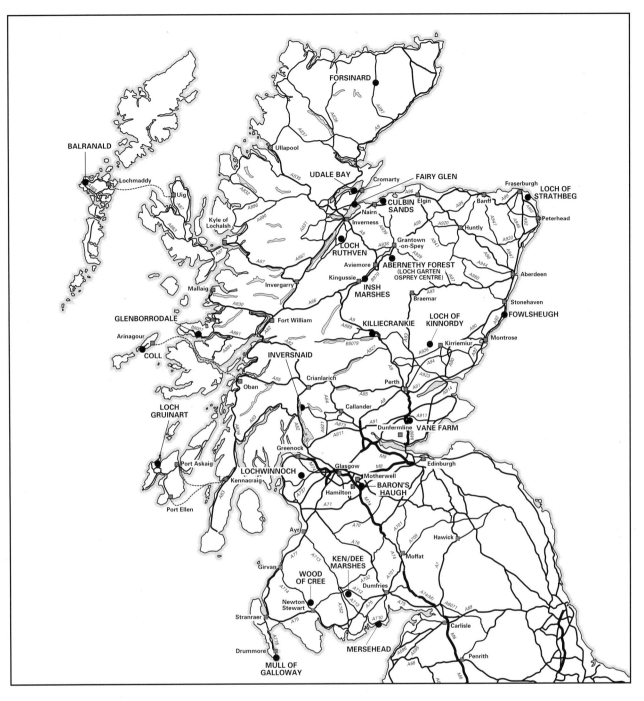

SCOTLAND

Balranald, Western Isles

NF/706707

Balranald is famous for its corncrakes, one of Europe's most endangered species. The visitor centre provides an ideal place to listen for the birds' calling. Machair, a habitat unique to north-west Scotland, occupies much of the nature reserve. It is created by wind-blown shellsand fertilising the underlying peat. Here masses of wildflowers and grasses mix with the corn, grown as winter feed for cattle and sheep. The machair supports huge numbers of breeding wading birds, such as dunlins, ringed plovers, lapwings and oystercatchers. Otters can also be seen in the freshwater lochs.

Baron's Haugh, Strathclyde
NS/7555552 ♿ **I P**

This is a typical marshland habitat with wigeons, teals, mallards, pochards and tufted ducks. Over 80 whooper swans on the nature reserve in the winter. Kingfishers and common sandpipers can be seen along the River Clyde which runs on the edge of the nature reserve.

Coll, Strathclyde
NM/1554 I P

Over 1,200 ha (2,960 acre) of shellsand beaches, sand dunes, machair, low intensity agricultural land and moorland make up this nature reserve. From May to August, the nature reserve is of prime importance for the corncrake. Other birds, including lapwings, snipe and dunlins, nest and feed on the damp machair. The sand dunes are Sites of Special Scientific Interest (SSSI) for their incredible richness of flowers, including many species of orchid. The surrounding sea has a wide range of seabirds and patient watchers may spot otters, seals, dolphins and whales.

Culbin Sands, Highland/Moray
NH/901573 P

Overlooking the Moray Firth, Culbin Sands forms one of the largest shingle and dune bars in Britain, behind which there is an extensive saltmarsh. Primarily important for wintering birds, there can be large numbers of seaducks offshore – long-tailed ducks and both common and velvet scoters – and bar-tailed godwits, oystercatchers and knots flock at high tide. Much of the nature reserve is remote, unspoilt and largely undisturbed.

Fairy Glen, Black Isle, Highland
NH/735579 P

This steep-sided valley of broadleaved woodland has a burn running through it. A pleasant walk takes you through mature woodland up the Rosemarkie Burn, where dippers are common and grey wagtails are usually seen. There are tumbling waterfalls and a quiet mill pond. Great-spotted woodpeckers and treecreepers inhabit the wood and in springtime, there are many woodland flowers.

C H Gomersall (RSPB Images)

Forsinard Nature Reserve

Forsinard, Highland
NC/892426 I P 🚶🚶

In the heart of the internationally important Flow Country, this nature reserve has over 7,000 ha (17,000 acres) of pool-studded, deep blanket peatland. Birds which can be seen include golden plovers, dunlins, greenshanks, merlins and hen harriers. A self-guided flagstone footpath threads its way through hundreds of bog pools teaming with sundews, bogbeans, dragonflies and other insects. Regular guided walks (which fit with train times) along with the visitor centre and its elevated bog pools, tell the 7,000-year old story of the peatlands. Many birds can be seen from the road which runs through the nature reserve and good views of the bogs can be had from the train which stops right outside the visitor centre.

Fowlsheugh, Grampian
NO/876805 P

These spectacular seabird cliffs support one of the largest seabird colonies on mainland Britain. Kittiwakes, guillemots and razorbills breed in huge numbers and puffins can also be seen. Fulmars, shags and herring gulls nest in smaller numbers. Bottle-nosed and white-beaked dolphins are seen offshore occasionally. Boat trips are organised from May to July.

Glenborrodale, Strathclyde
NM/601608 NM/593619 I P

On the rugged Ardnamurchan peninsula, Glenborrodale is an ancient oakwood on the shore of Loch Sunart. It is particularly important for the rich variety of mosses and lichens that live on the rocks and trees. In spring, wood warblers can be seen, along with a range of woodland birds. There is always a chance of seeing otters along the shore and seals are common. On the nature trail you can see young birch and oak – by reducing grazing, we are allowing young trees to survive and the woodland to extend.

Insh Marshes, Highland
NH/775998 I P

Insh Marshes are a wetland of international importance. Each winter and spring, the strath (or valley) is repeatedly covered with floodwater from the River Spey. The best times to visit are November to June. In springtime, you can see the largest population of breeding goldeneyes in Britain. Eight kinds of wader nest and hundreds of lapwings, snipe, curlews and redshanks fill the air with their display calls. Spotted crakes also breed. In winter, hundreds of whooper swans and greylag geese from Iceland visit the marshes and hen harriers roost. Wetland wildflowers are abundant and varied. For example, 28 species of sedge (some very rare) can be seen in summer, plus orchids in the meadows. Scotch argus butterflies are common. Red squirrels and otters can also be seen.

Inversnaid, Central
NN/337088 I P

The nature reserve is located on a steep slope rising up from Loch Lomond through deciduous woodland to a craggy ridge, beyond which lies open moorland. The resident woodland birds are joined in summer by migrants such as pied flycatchers, redstarts, wood warblers and tree pipits. Buzzards nest on the crags, while black grouse can be found on the woodland edge and moorland. Dippers, grey wagtails and common sandpipers breed on the loch shore and along the burns. There are excellent communities of ferns, lichens and bryophytes. Look out too for signs of badgers, pine martens and deer.

Ken/Dee Marshes, Dumfries & Galloway
NX/637763 I P

This is a diverse wetland and broadleaved woodland site where marshes have been increased in size since 1935 due to hydro-electric operations. The major interest is wintering wildfowl, including internationally important numbers of Greenland white-fronted geese and nationally important numbers of greylag geese. Breeding birds include good numbers of wildfowl, and woodland birds include redstarts, pied flycatchers and willow tits. Mammals include red squirrels, harvest mice and otters. The site is important for a range of plants and invertebrates.

Killiecrankie, Tayside
NN/907627 I P

This nature reserve is steep and hilly, with spectacular views all around. Oak and birch woodland, moorland and pasture are the main habitats, supporting a wide variety of birds, including buzzards, ravens, wood warblers, redstarts, tree pipits, curlews and black grouse. The plant life is very rich, especially in the mires, which contain northern and early marsh orchids, Scottish asphodel and broad-leaved cotton-grass. Wood vetch and many different ferns are among the species to be seen along the woodland paths. Dark green and small pearl-bordered fritillaries and Scotch argus butterflies fly in the summer; roe deer are common and red squirrels are still present.

Loch Gruinart, Islay, Strathclyde
NR/275672 P 🏃🏃

Loch Gruinart Nature Reserve has a wide range of Hebridean habitats, from wet grassland, marsh and meadows to mudflats, saltmarsh and heather moorland. The nature reserve is internationally important for its wintering populations of barnacle and white-fronted geese. During spring, there are hundreds of breeding waders including lapwings, redshanks and snipe and the nights resound to the call of the corncrake. Hen harriers nest on the moor and hunting eagles and peregrines prey all year round on the rich wildlife the reserve supports.

Loch of Kinnordy, Angus

NO/361539 ♿ I P

This very attractive shallow loch, set among mires and willow scrub, supports large numbers of breeding birds. Black-necked and great crested grebes, shovelers, gadwalls, pochards, mallards and teals all nest, and the black-headed gull colony numbers several thousand pairs. Ospreys fish daily in the summer and marsh harriers are regular visitors. In some years, there is a large autumn roost of pink-footed geese, and goosanders and goldeneyes visit in the winter.

Loch Ruthven, Highland

NH/638281 P

Loch Ruthven is a beautiful Highland loch fringed by sedges and birchwoods, giving way to open moorland. The loch is the most important breeding site in Britain for the rare Slavonian grebe, one of our most beautiful breeding birds. The hide provides the perfect setting to watch the grebes without causing disturbance. Through the spring and summer, the birds court and pair, nest and raise young. Ospreys and black grouse can be seen.

C H Gomersall (RSPB Images)

Loch Ruthven Nature Reserve

Loch of Strathbeg, Aberdeenshire

NK/057581 ♿ I P ♟

The largest freshwater loch on the Grampian coast is separated from the sea by wide sand dunes and is bordered by freshwater fen, marsh, woodland and farmland. The Loch of Strathbeg is of international importance for wintering waterfowl including pink-footed geese and whooper swans. From the observation room, a good selection of waders can be seen, especially during migration periods. Breeding birds include Sandwich terns, water rails, shelducks, tufted ducks, lapwings, sedge and willow warblers. Roe deer, foxes, badgers and otters are all resident throughout the year. Of botanical interest, lesser butterfly orchids, coral-root orchids and grass of Parnassus occur annually.

Mersehead, Dumfries & Galloway

NX/025560 P

Sandwiched between the rolling Stewartry Hills and the Solway, this nature reserve is in an area rich in natural beauty, history and wildlife. It is designated part Site of Special Scientific Interest (SSSI), Ramsar site, Special Protection Area (SPA), Special Area of Conservation (SAC) and Environmentally Sensitive Area (ESA). The spectacle in winter is stunning, with up to 7,000 barnacle geese and several thousand ducks, including large numbers of wigeons, pintails and teals. This is complemented by increasing numbers of waders such as lapwings, oystercatchers and curlews in both spring and winter. The merse and dunes are well populated with moth and butterfly species. Roe deer, badgers, foxes and otters are resident throughout the year.

Mull of Galloway, Dumfries & Galloway

NX/157304. I P

The Mull of Galloway is the most southerly point in Scotland and the 85 m (276 ft) cliffs offer fine views out over the Solway and Irish Sea to the Isle of Man. The cliffs support the largest mainland seabird colony in the region, with guillemots, razorbills, fulmars, shags and a few puffins. Around the lighthouse, a small area of maritime heath survives, and many of the cliff-top plants are nationally and regionally scarce, including species such as spring squill, purple milk vetch and sea bladderwort. To the east, lies the small rocky outcrop of Scare Rocks, which is another RSPB nature reserve and supports 2,000 pairs of breeding gannets.

Udale Bay, Highland
NH/712651 ♿ P

Lying on the Cromarty Firth, Udale Bay is an extensive area of mudflats, saltmarsh and wet grassland. From early autumn through to April, the nature reserve supports large numbers of wildfowl and wading birds. Best visited within an hour of high tide, there can be spectacular views of flocks of waders. The nature reserve holds up to 5,000 wigeons in autumn, feeding on the rich beds of eelgrass that grow in the bay. Late summer is a good time to see fishing ospreys.

Wood of Cree, Dumfries & Galloway
NX/382708 I P

The Wood of Cree is the most extensive and best example of ancient woodland remaining in southern Scotland. It is situated on an escarpment slope overlooking the River Cree, with its associated floodplain mire and willow carr and two small grazing meadows. On the higher ground, the wood grades into open scrub and plantation with a mixture of heath and wet and dry grassland, creating an attractive mosaic. The nature reserve also includes two smaller ancient woodlands to the west of the River Cree, Glenhapple and Knockville. The site is of regional importance for breeding wood warblers and pied flycatchers.

ORKNEY RESERVES

Birsay Moors and Cottasgarth
HY/368187 ♿ I

This large, West Mainland nature reserve, covering 2,360 ha (5,830 acres), consists largely of moorland, but the beautiful, herb-rich valley mire at Durkadale has developed extensive areas of willow scrub and reedbeds, both scarce habitats on Orkney. The nature reserve is particularly important for breeding raptors such as hen harriers, merlins, ground-nesting kestrels and short-eared owls. Arctic and great skuas, red-throated divers, curlews and an increasing population of whimbrels also breed. The Orkney vole is particularly abundant in rank grass.

Copinsay
HY/610010 I

This uninhabited island lies two miles off the coast of East Mainland. Copinsay and its three adjacent holms (islets connected to the main island at low tide) and the rock stack known as the Horse were purchased as a memorial to the naturalist James Fisher. Copinsay lies like a great wedge with almost a mile of vertical cliffs up to 76 m (247 ft) high, facing south-east into the North Sea. Counts of seabirds in 1994 gave totals of 1,922 pairs of fulmars, 3,750 kittiwake nests, 20,440 guillemots and 1,390 pairs of great black-backed gulls. Sadly, peregrines and corncrakes have not bred for several years, but we hope that with careful management the latter may return.

Hobbister
HY/396070 I

This 780 ha (1,920 acre) nature reserve lies 5 km (3 miles) south-west of Kirkwall in the West Mainland. It is primarily heather moorland, but has a great variety of other habitats such as bog, fen, low cliffs and at Waulkmill Bay, saltmarsh and tidal sandflats. Having remained virtually unburned and ungrazed for many years, the nature reserve has one of the best moorland bird

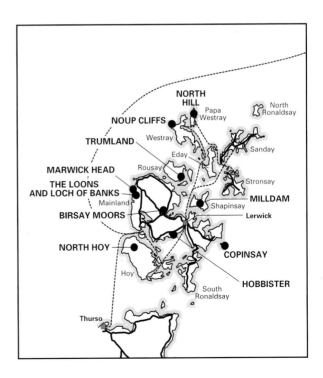

communities left in Orkney, with high densities of meadow pipits, skylarks, twites and curlews. The nature reserve is also important for birds of prey with several pairs of hen harriers, merlins, kestrels and short-eared owls.

Wigeon

The Loons and Loch of Banks

HY/246242 **P**

In Orkney, marshland is a habitat constantly under the threat of drainage. With a recently purchased extension at the Loch of Banks, the RSPB now owns 81 ha (200 acres) of what is, by common consent, the finest remaining marsh in Orkney. The Loons, technically a basin mire, is completely flooded in the winter and remains wet in the summer. Old peat cuttings and low-level cattle grazing ensure excellent conditions both for interesting plants and birds. Eight species of duck breed including one quarter of Britain's breeding population of pintails. Very high densities of breeding waders ensure an unforgettable experience, especially during the spring when they are in full and noisy display.

Marwick Head

HY/229242 **I**

Of all the seabird colonies, Marwick Head is the most accessible and no less spectacular than others such as Copinsay or the Noup Cliffs on Westray. The nature reserve lies in the north-west corner of West Mainland just 2 km (1 mile) from The Loons

Nature Reserve. The 86 m (280 ft) high Old Red Sandstone cliffs are home to nearly 8,000 pairs of kittiwakes and 36,000 guillemots. There are also good numbers of fulmars and razorbills and even a few puffins for the observant watcher. Such northern specialities as ravens, rock doves and twites may also be seen here.

Milldam, Shapinsay

HY/481177 ♿ **I**

Although only 16 ha (39 acres) in area, this small nature reserve has six species of breeding duck and five species of breeding wader. Ducks include breeding wigeons, shovelers and pintails. Among the waders, redshanks are perhaps at a higher density here than anywhere else on Orkney, with up to 15 pairs. The sight and sound on a fine spring day is hard to beat and over 700 pairs of black-headed gulls certainly add to the atmosphere. The Milldam is also important for wintering wildfowl with over 100 whooper swans and hundreds of ducks and geese.

North Hill, Papa Westray

HY/223034 **I**

The low cliffs on the east side of the nature reserve, known as the Fowl Craig, were one of the last breeding sites in Britain of the great auk – the last was killed in 1813. These cliffs now hold small colonies of kittiwakes, razorbills and guillemots. Wide, rock viewing platforms offer superb, close views. High concentrations of the stunning black guillemot can be seen nesting under boulders and flagstones. However, it is the maritime heath which is the greatest attraction with its carpets of dwarf shrubs and flowers including the very rare Scottish primrose, *Primula scotica,* and, of course, the large colonies of arctic terns and arctic skuas.

Arctic terns

North Hoy, Orkney

HY/39023 ▌

The 3,926 ha (9,700 acre) nature reserve simply has everything: moorland, spectacular 340 m (1,100 ft) high cliffs, the Old Man of Hoy, the most northerly native wood at Berriedale, crags and gullies peppered with arctic/alpine flowers, superb scenery, mountain hares and birds galore. There are also hundreds of pairs of great skuas (or bonxies), red-throated divers, seabird colonies, seven species of breeding raptor, grouse, waders such as golden plovers and dunlins, and high densities of songbirds such as stonechats and wheatears.

Noup Cliffs, Westray

HY/392500 ▌

At the north-west tip of Westray, the Noup Cliffs have one of the largest seabird colonies in the British Isles. A 2.4 km (1.5 mile) stretch of cliffs holds 44,500 guillemots, 13,000 kittiwake nests, 1,500 razorbills and 1,130 pairs of fulmars. In 1994, 130 puffins were also counted for good measure.

Trumland, Rousay

HY/427276 ▌ ♦♦

This 433 ha (1,000 acre) nature reserve comprises moorland similar in character to the moors of Orkney Mainland. Breeding birds include red-throated divers, peregrines, merlins, short-eared owls, golden plovers and both species of skua. The twin summits of Knitchen Hill and Blotchnie Field, which can be reached by following the nature trail, afford spectacular views over almost the whole of Orkney.

SHETLAND

Fetlar

HU/604916

Most of the nature reserve consists of grassy heathland encompassing the summits of Vord Hill and Stackaberg. It is bordered by high sea cliffs and boulder shores to the north and crofting areas to the south. The island has almost all of Britain's breeding red-necked phalaropes and large numbers of whimbrels, skuas and terns. On the shores, common and grey seals and otters can be seen.

Loch of Spiggie, Mainland

HU/373176

A shallow freshwater loch covers most of the nature reserve. The loch is separated from the sea by sand dunes and from the neighbouring Loch of Brow by a marsh. As many as 300 whooper swans winter here as well as greylag geese.

Lumbister, Mainland

HU/509974

This vast nature reserve covers habitats ranging from undulating moorland of heather and bog to the rocky shore of Whale Firth. Red-throated divers, eiders, merlins, skuas, golden plovers, curlews, puffins, rock doves and guillemots breed.

Sumburgh Head, Mainland

HU/407078

The spectacular sea cliffs and stacks are easily accessible by car and can be viewed in safety from behind stone walls and fences. Thousands of puffins, guillemots and other seabirds can be seen.

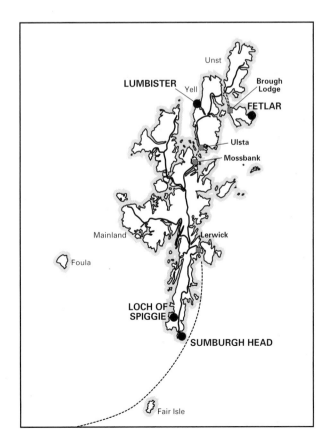

NORTHERN IRELAND

Lower Lough Erne Islands, Co Fermanagh

H/009603 P ⚲⚲

Over 40 islands on Lower Lough Erne make up this nature reserve, some of which are managed for important populations of breeding waders – curlews, lapwings, redshanks and snipe. Other species include the Sandwich tern, shoveler, teal, mallard, great crested and little grebe, and whooper swan in winter. Mammals include otters, badgers and pine martens.

Lough Foyle, Co Londonderry

C/545237 P

The nature reserve comprises an expansive area of intertidal mudflats, shell ridges and mussel beds below the high water mark. This zone is rich in eelgrass which provides the main food for thousands of migrant brent geese and wigeons. The surrounding arable land hosts over 1,000 wintering whooper swans and smaller numbers of Bewick's swans and grey geese. Many waders also use the Lough including wintering bar-tailed godwits, dunlins, knots and golden plovers and autumn passage little stints and curlew sandpipers. In recent years, over 100 Slavonian grebes, along with great northern and red-throated divers, have been noted off the Myroe Bank. Otters frequent the many drains behind the seawall and Irish hares can be seen in the fields in late winter/early spring. The best time to visit is October through to early December.

Portmore Lough, Co Antrim

T/107685 P

The nature reserve consists of lowland wet meadows, scrub and reedbed on the western shore of Portmore Lough (also known as Lough Beg). It is important for wintering greylag geese, whooper swans and a variety of wildfowl. Breeding birds include curlews, gadwalls, tree sparrows, sedge and grasshopper warblers.

Rathlin Island Cliffs, Co Antrim

D/093516

High chalk and basalt cliffs fringe the east-west arm of the island with offshore stacks at the west end. These cliffs and stacks are the site of Northern Ireland's finest seabird breeding colony. The West Lighthouse Platform offers magnificent views of guillemots, razorbills, puffins and fulmars. Access to the platform is permitted under the supervision of the RSPB warden. The best time to visit is late May to mid-July. The rough pasture, maritime heath, loughs and freshwater marshes of the island support a wide variety of birds including ravens, buzzards and peregrines and flowering plants, such as heath spotted orchid and pyramidal bugle. Grey and common seals may be seen basking on the rocks.

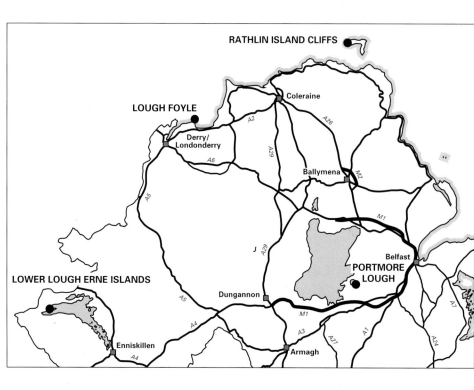

Index

The alphabetical arrangement is letter by letter.

Numbers in italics refer to photographs and illustrations.

Numbers in bold refer to main descriptions of reserves.